Cupcake

Coloring Book

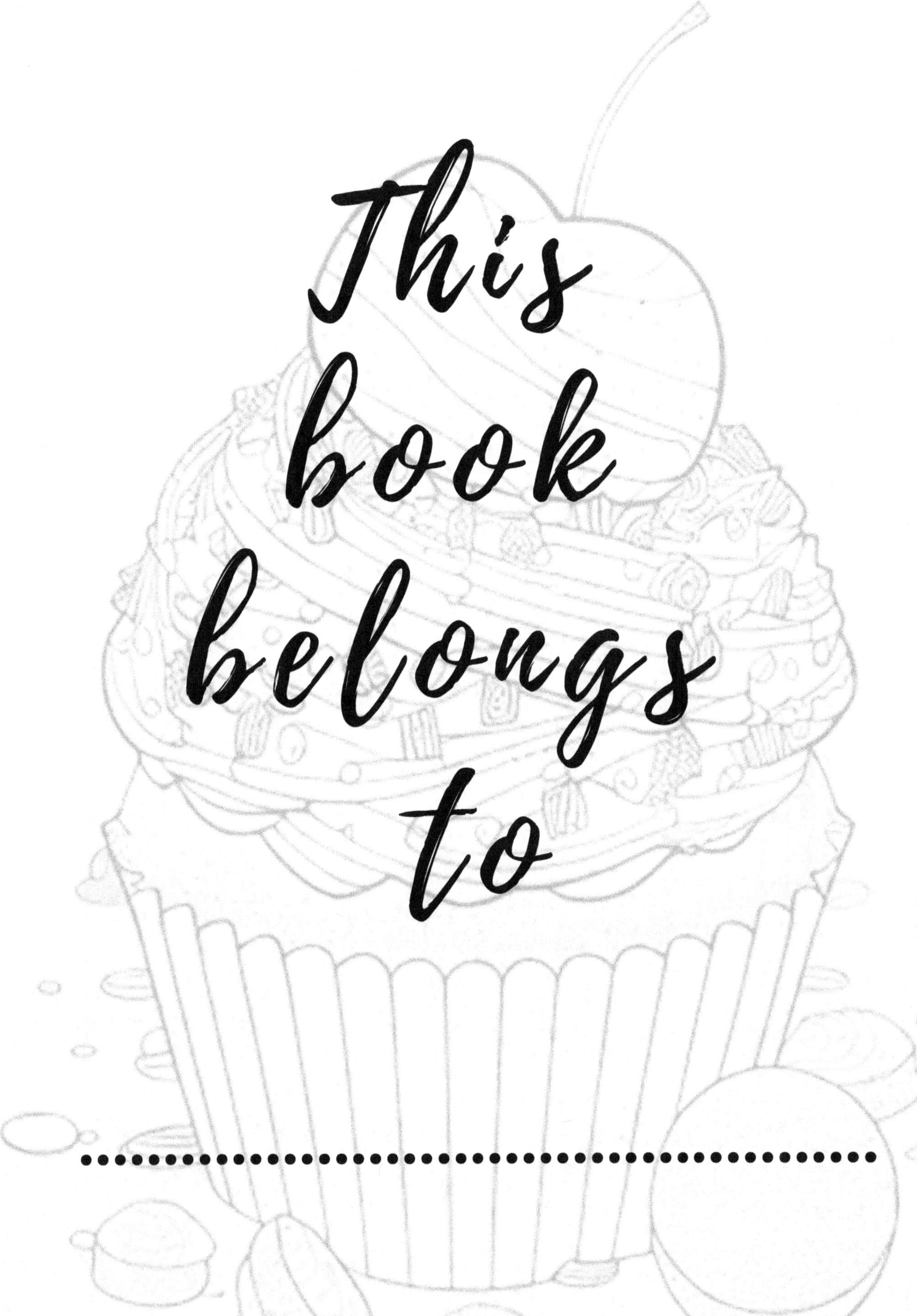

This book belongs to

....

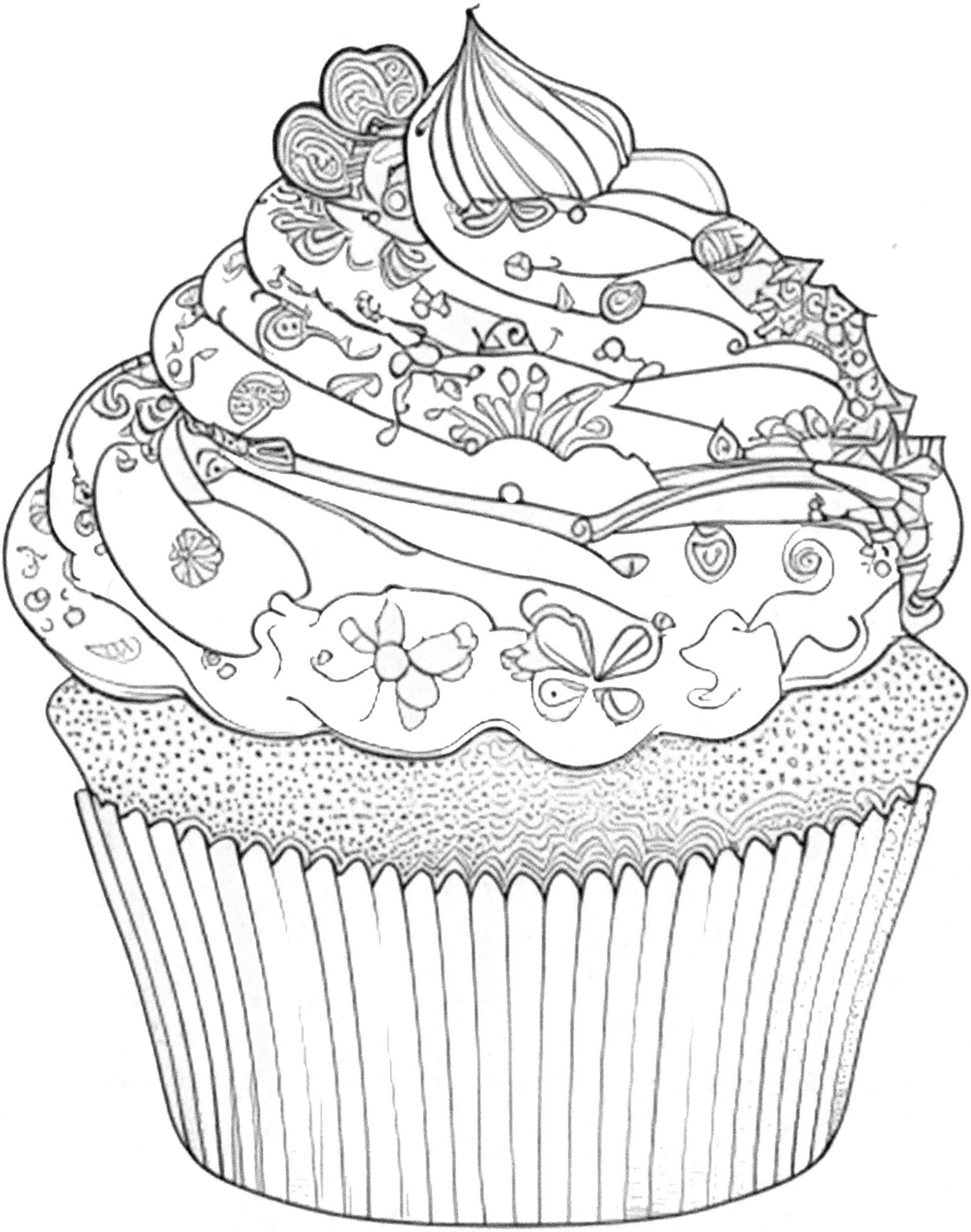

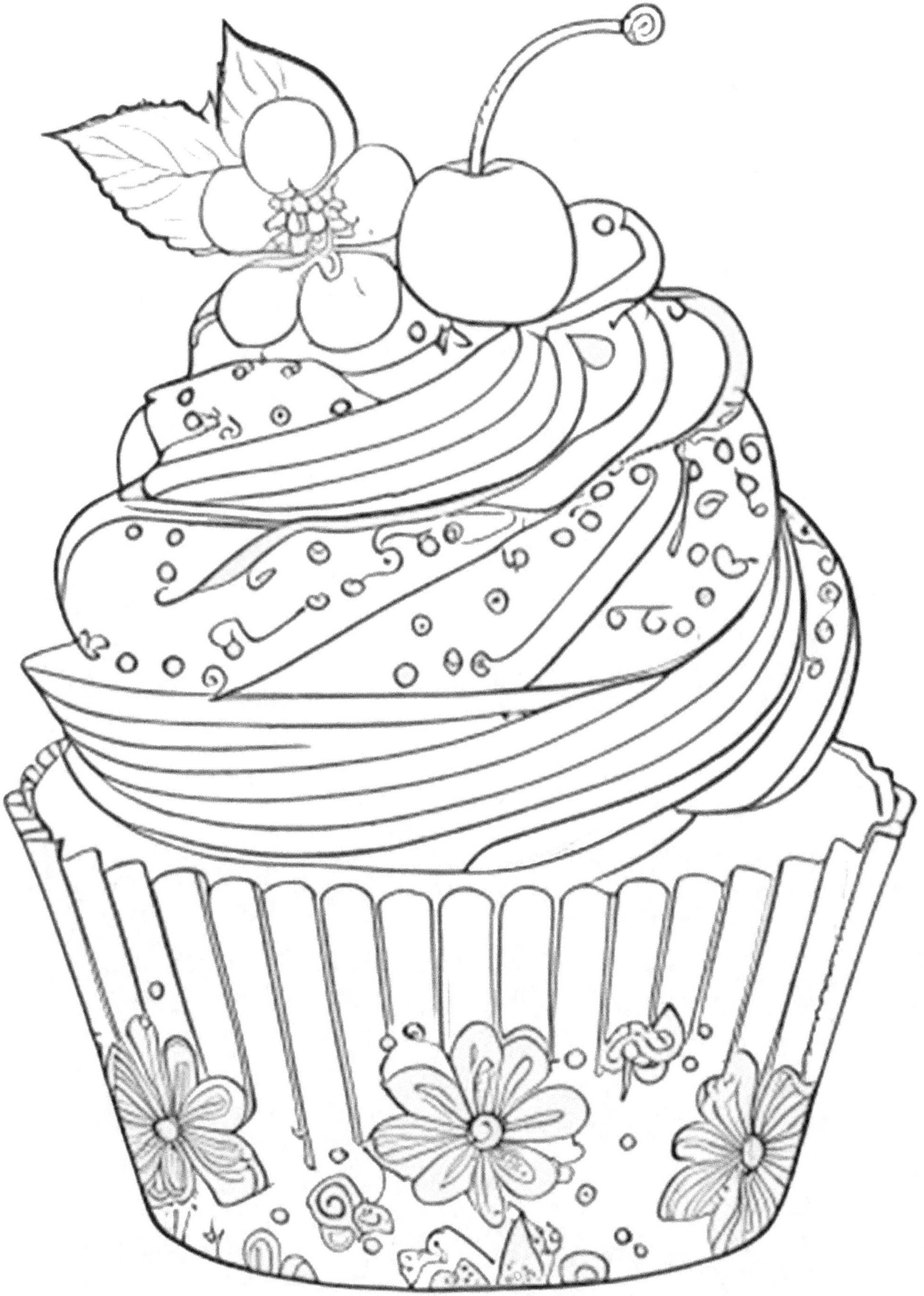

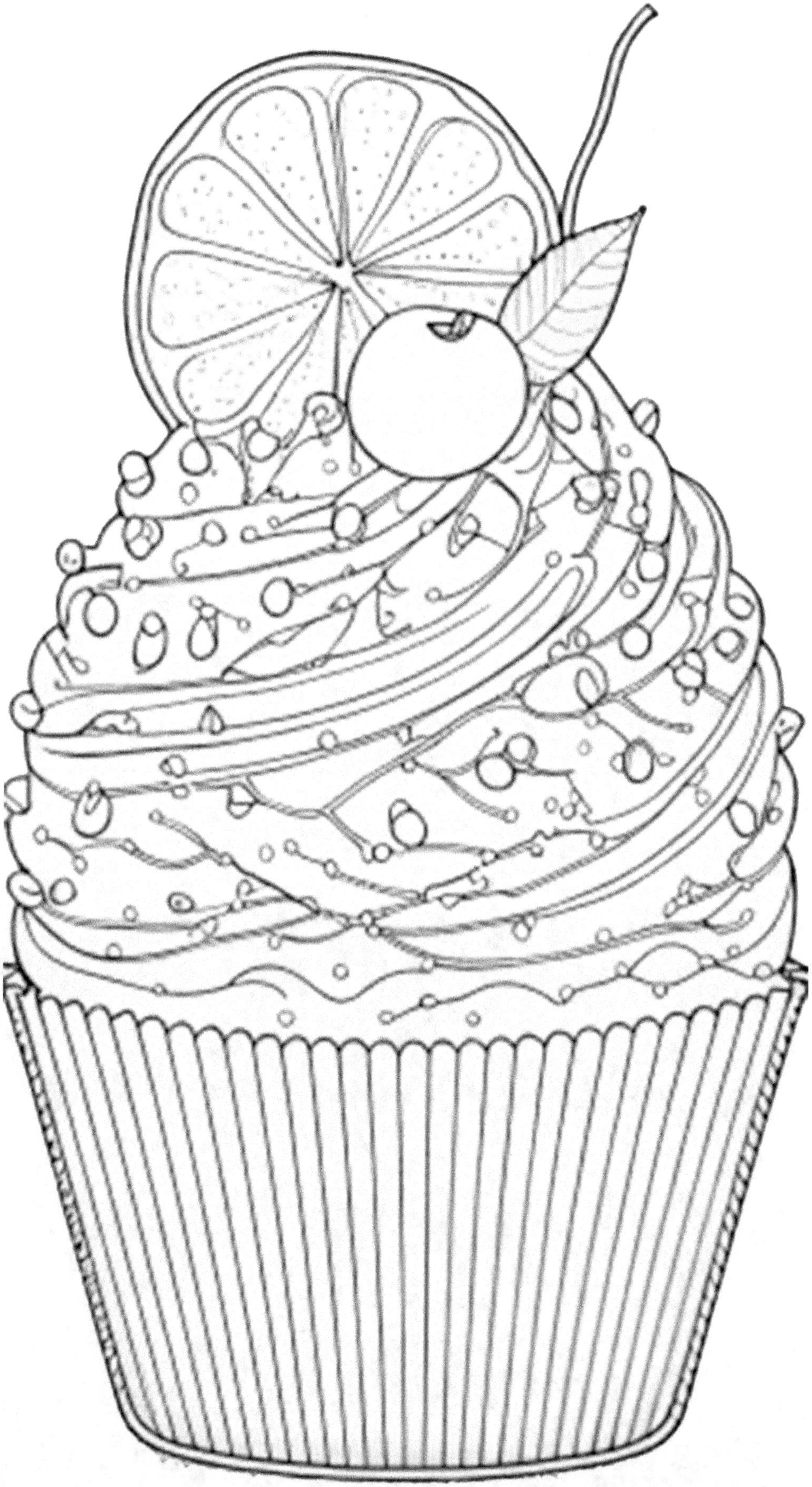

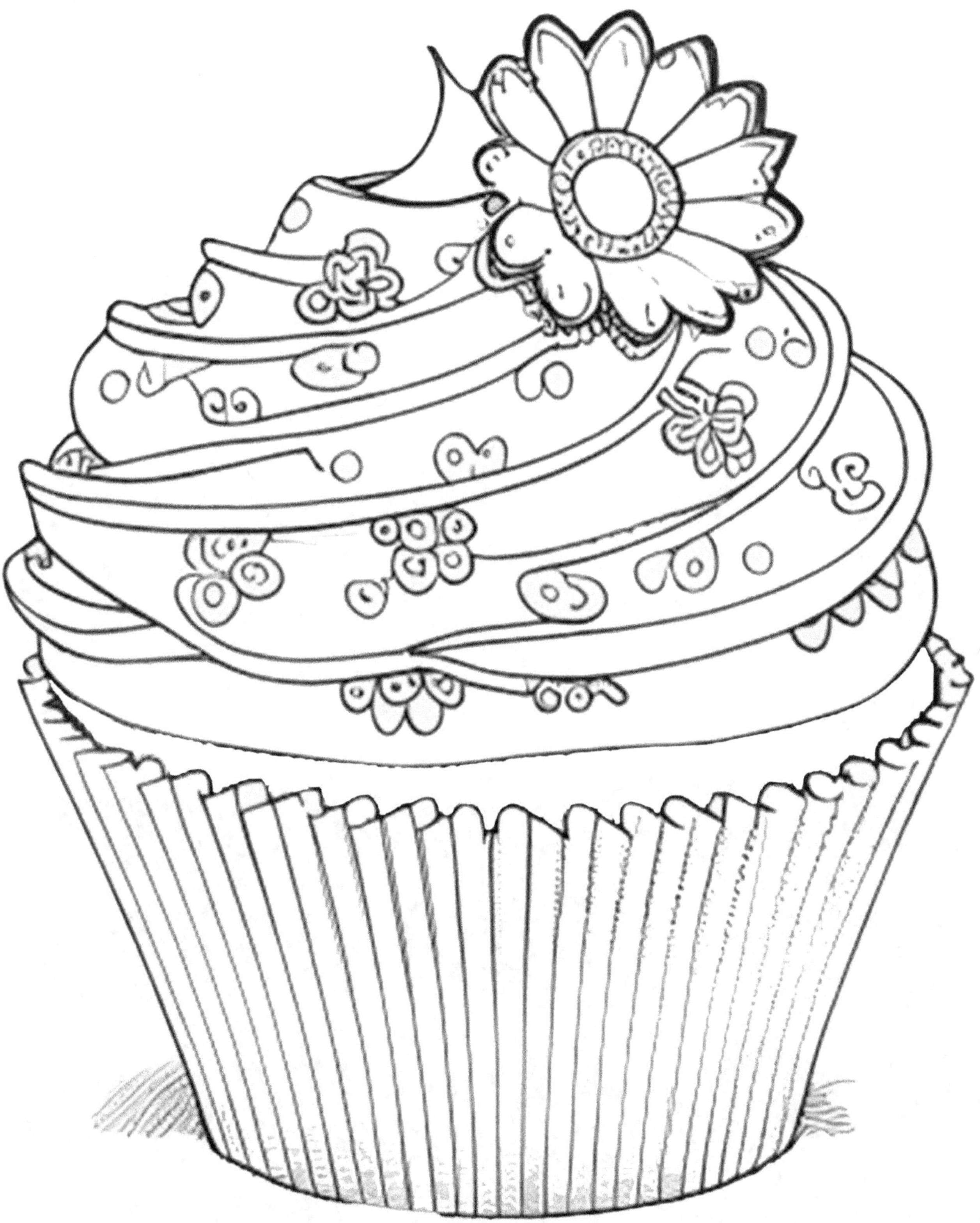

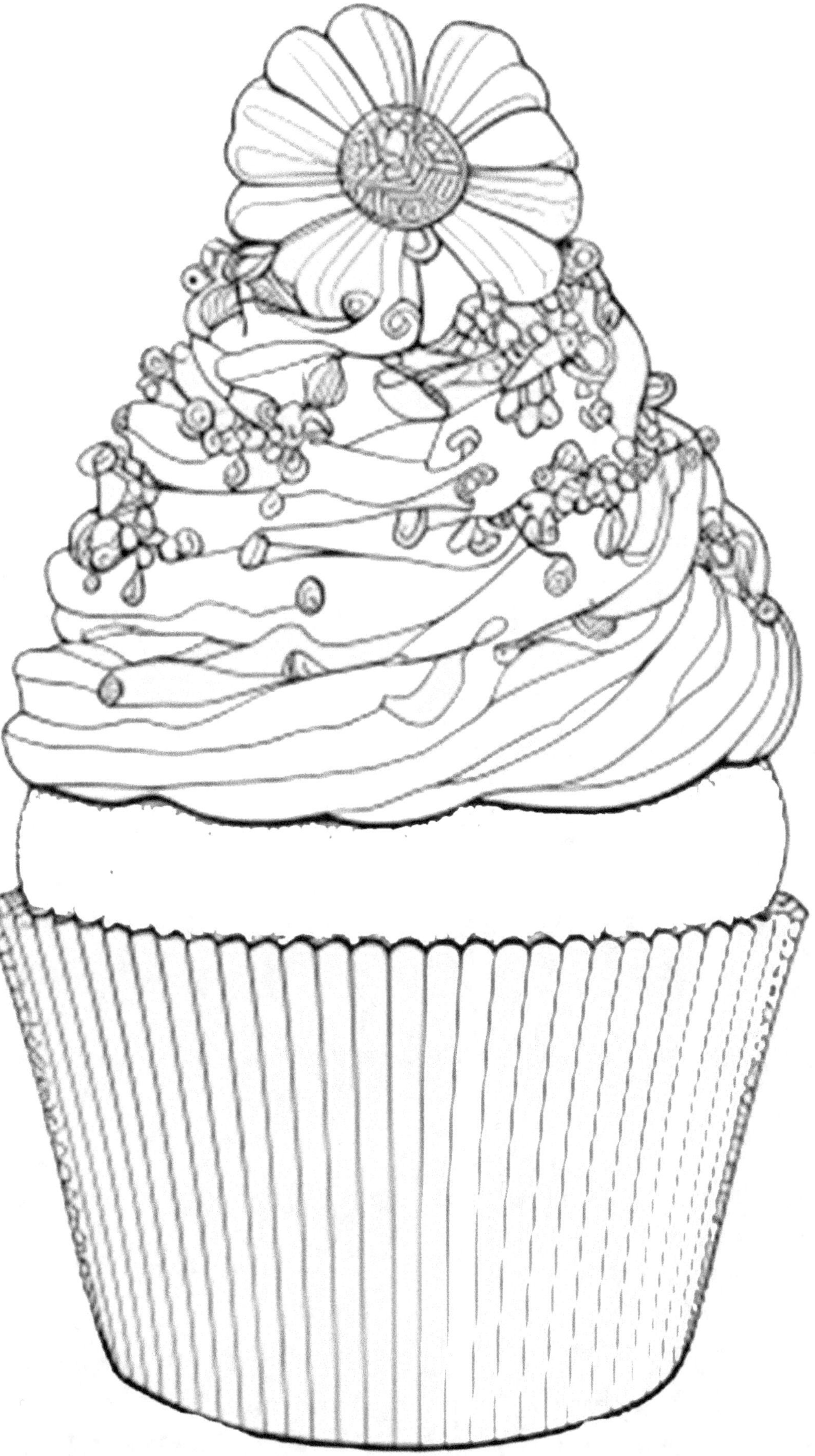

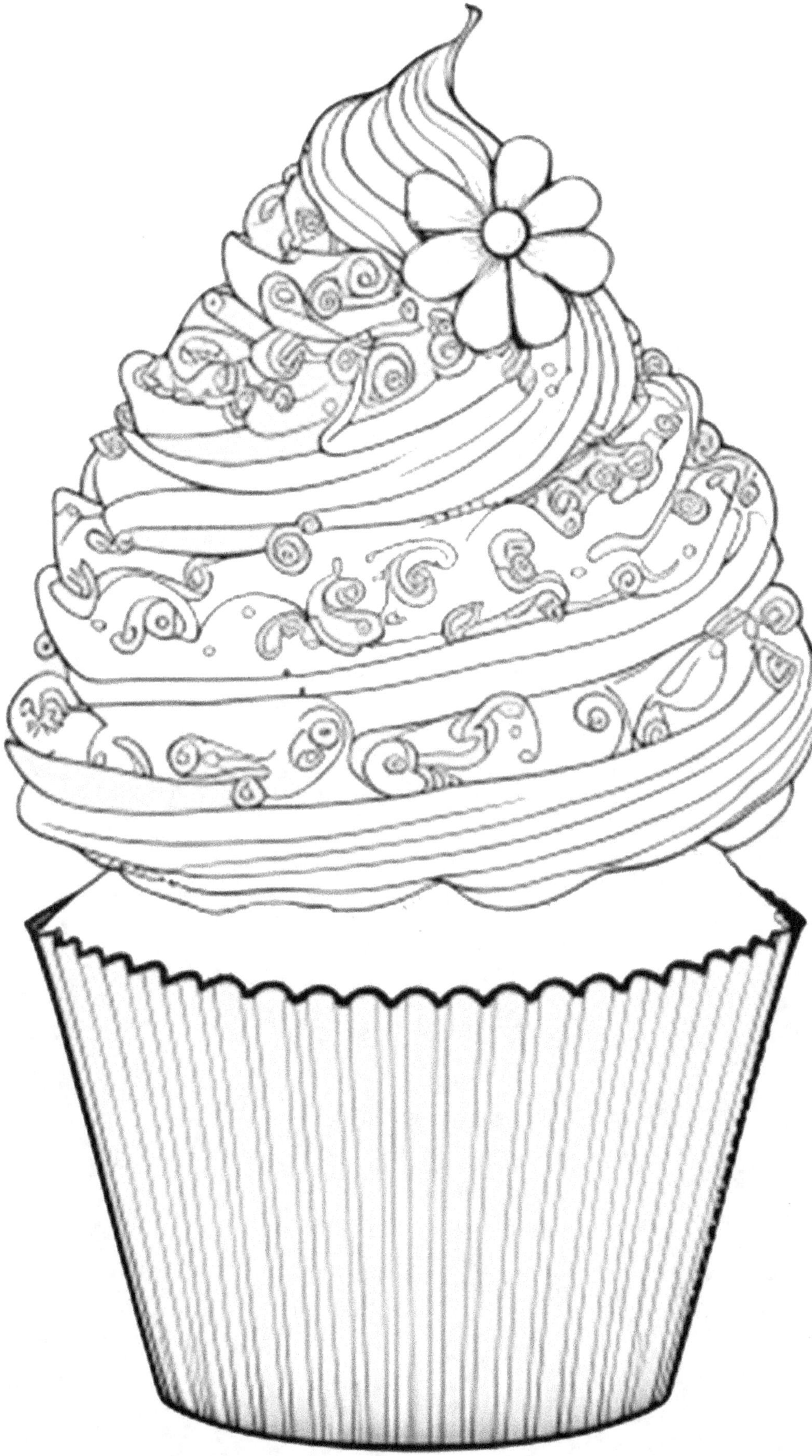

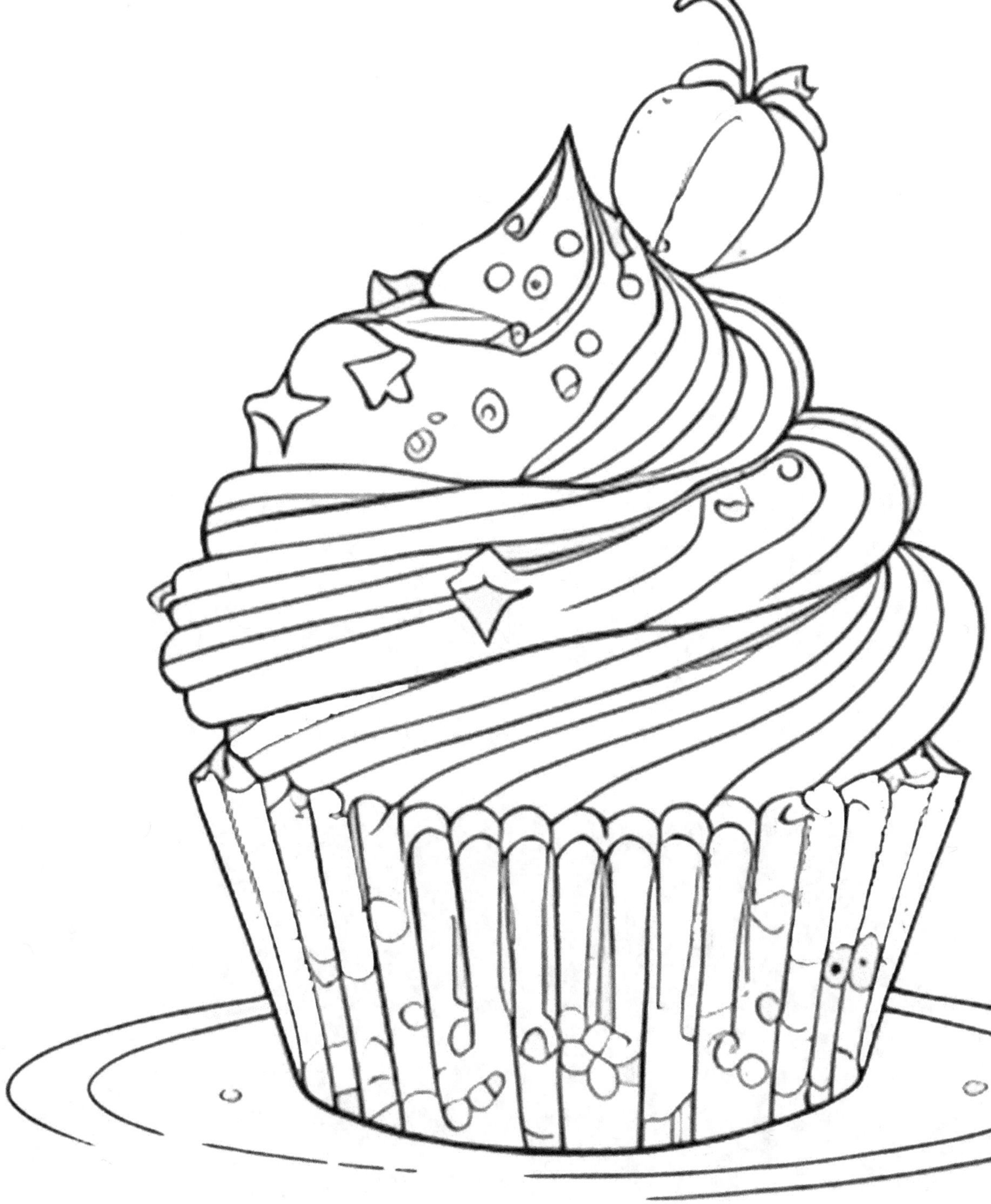

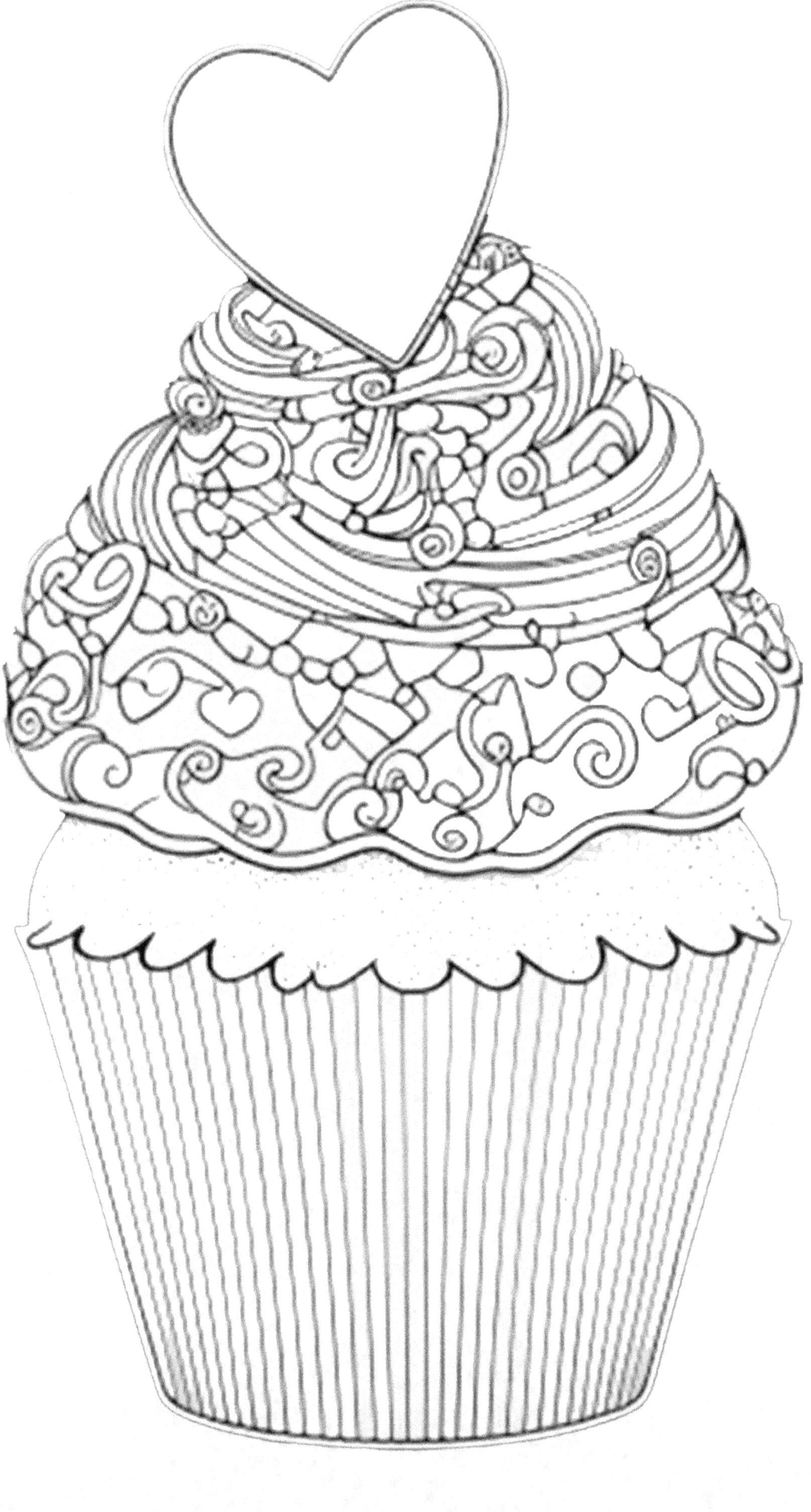

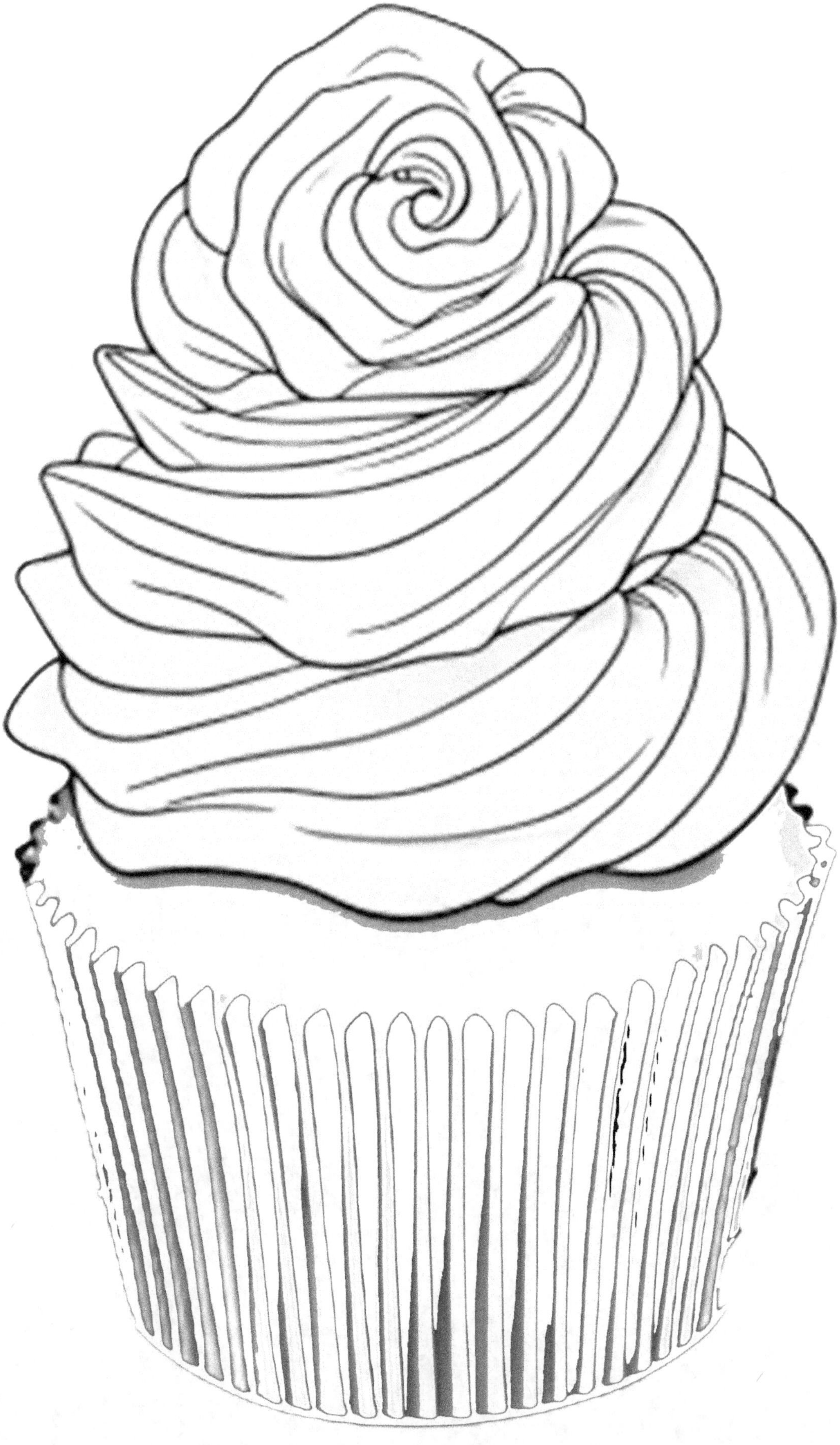

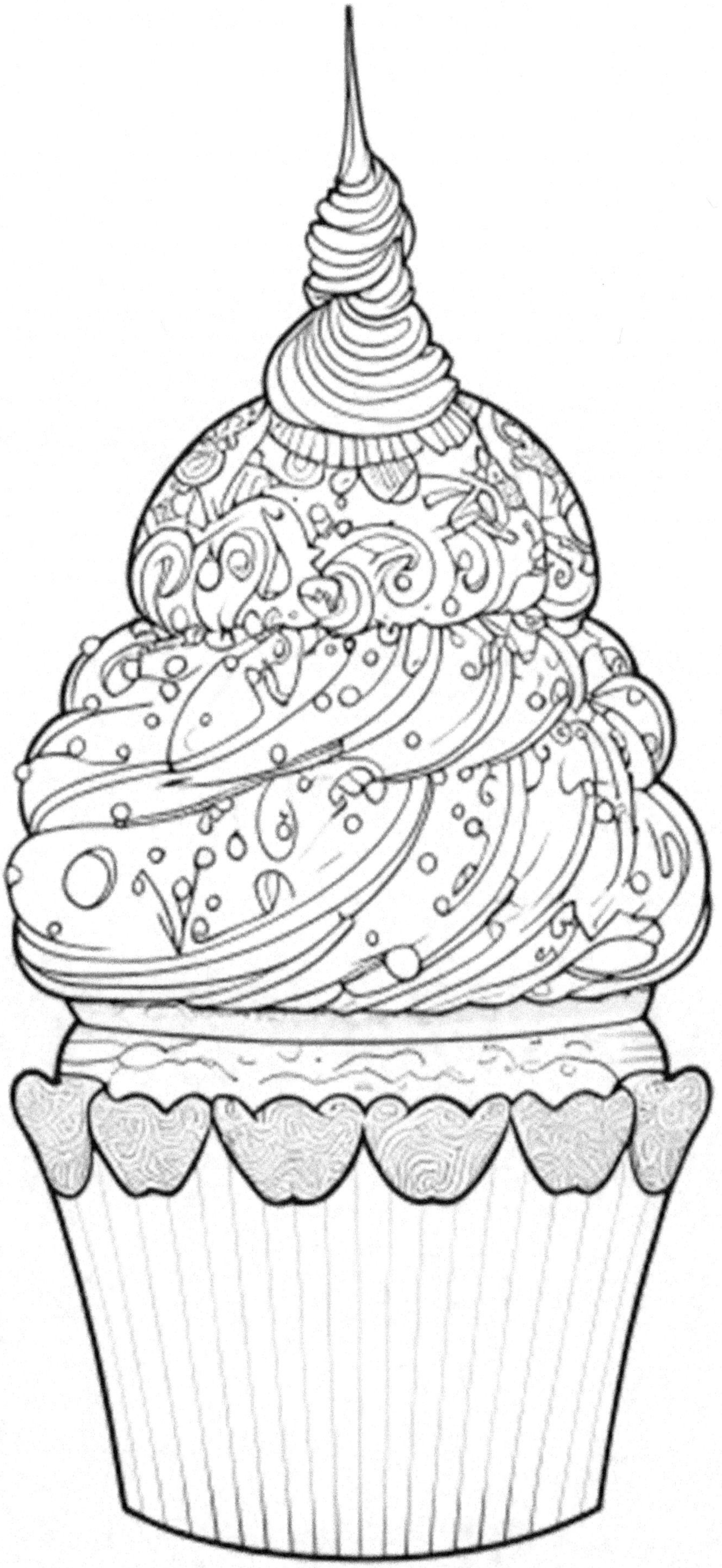

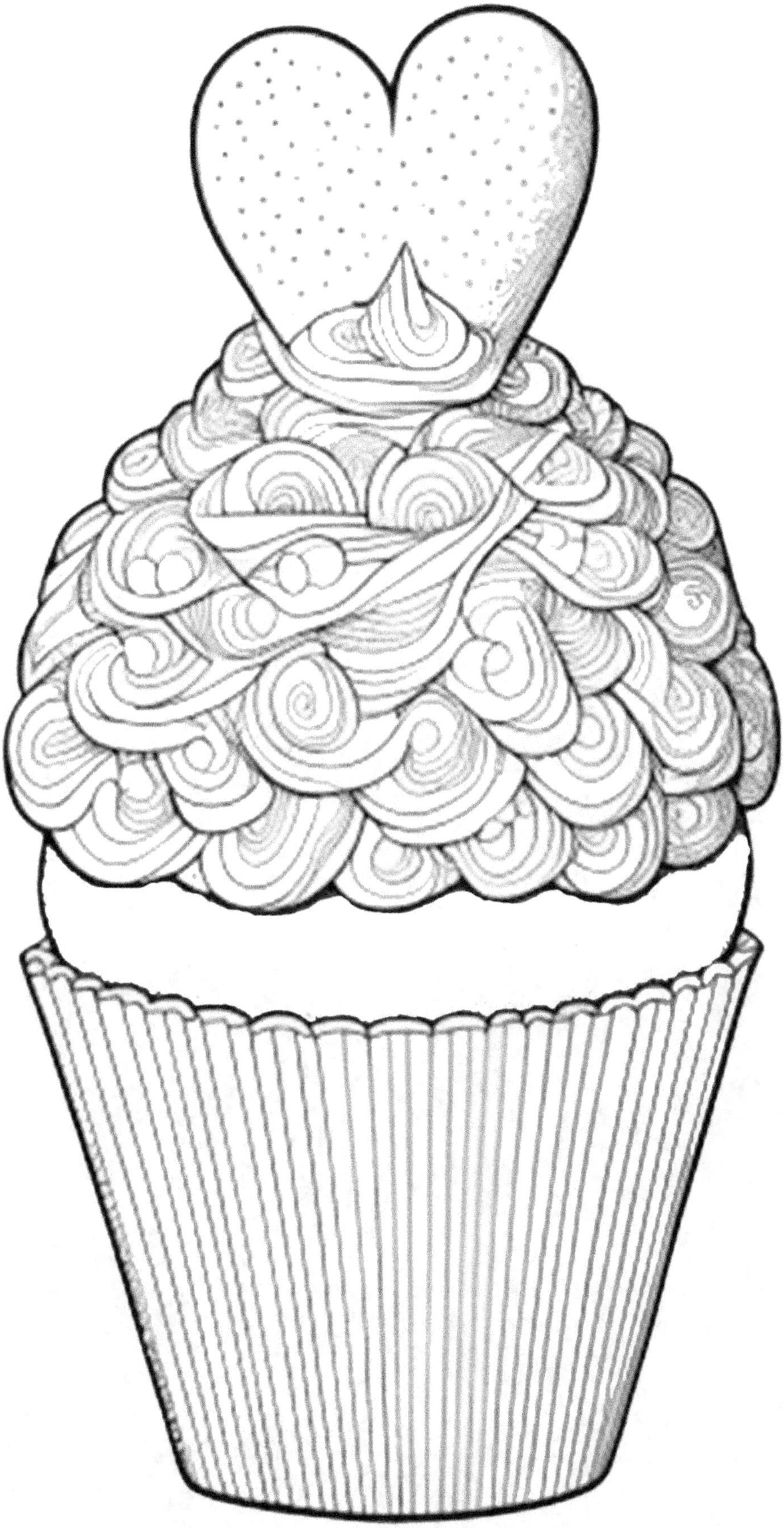

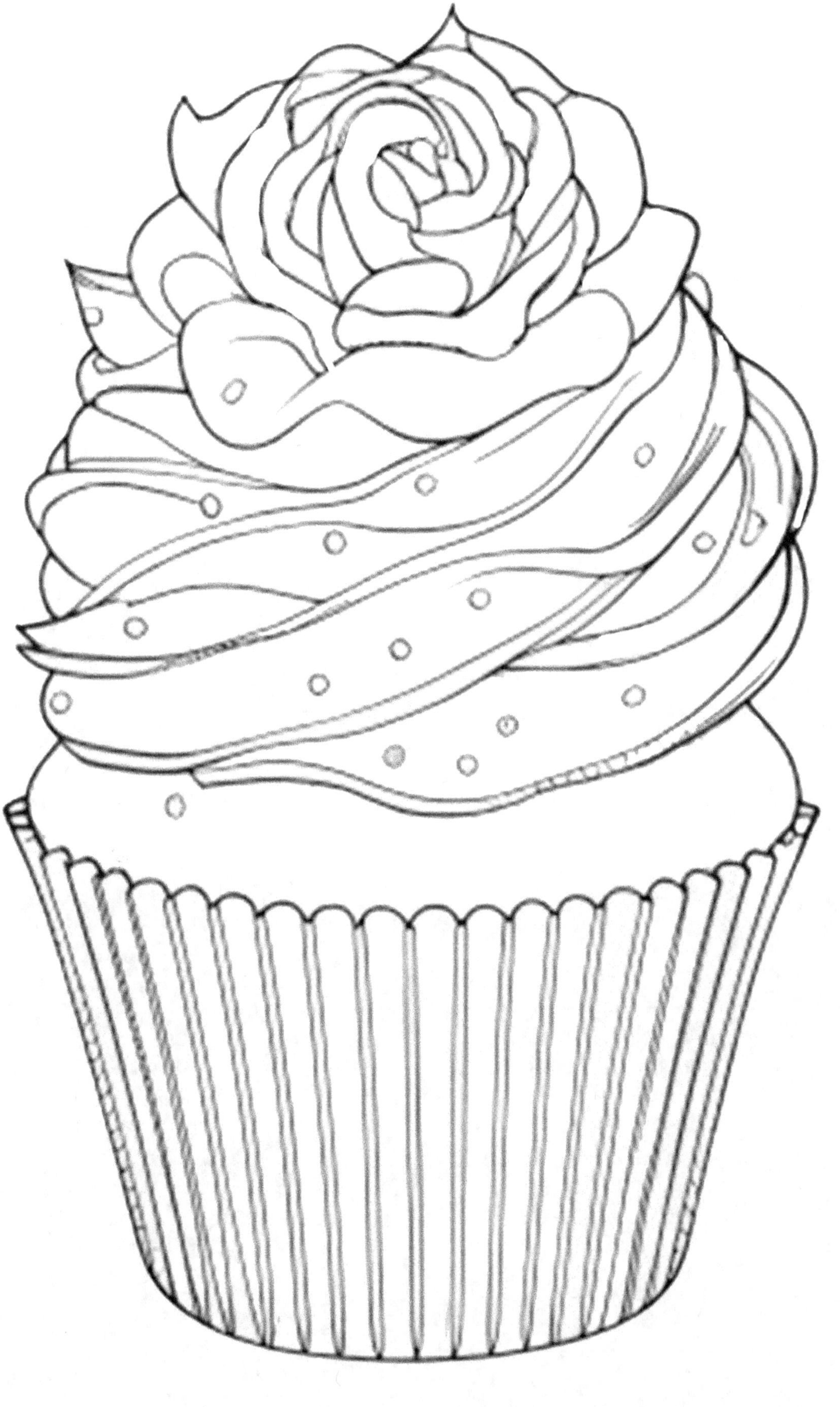

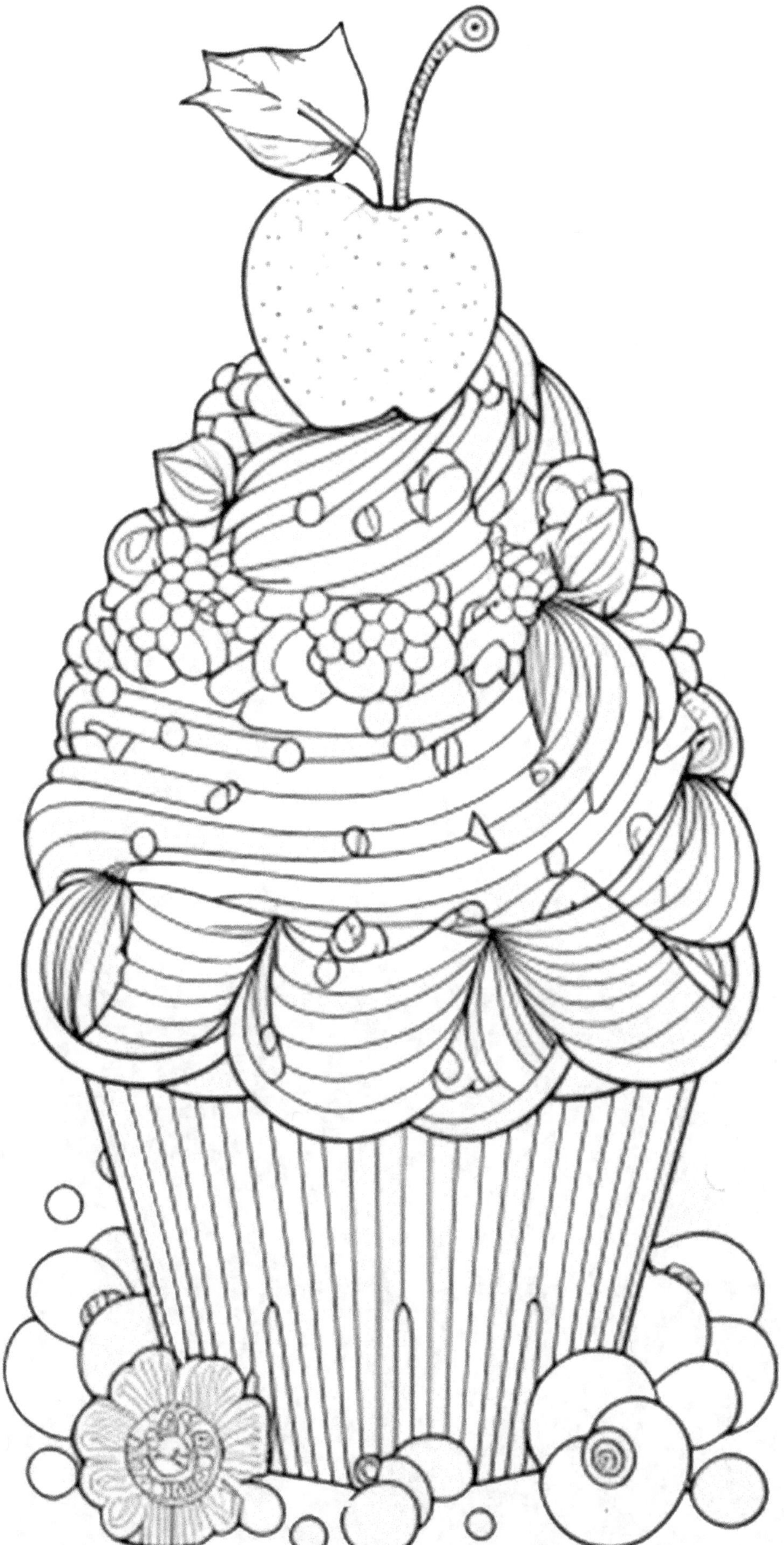

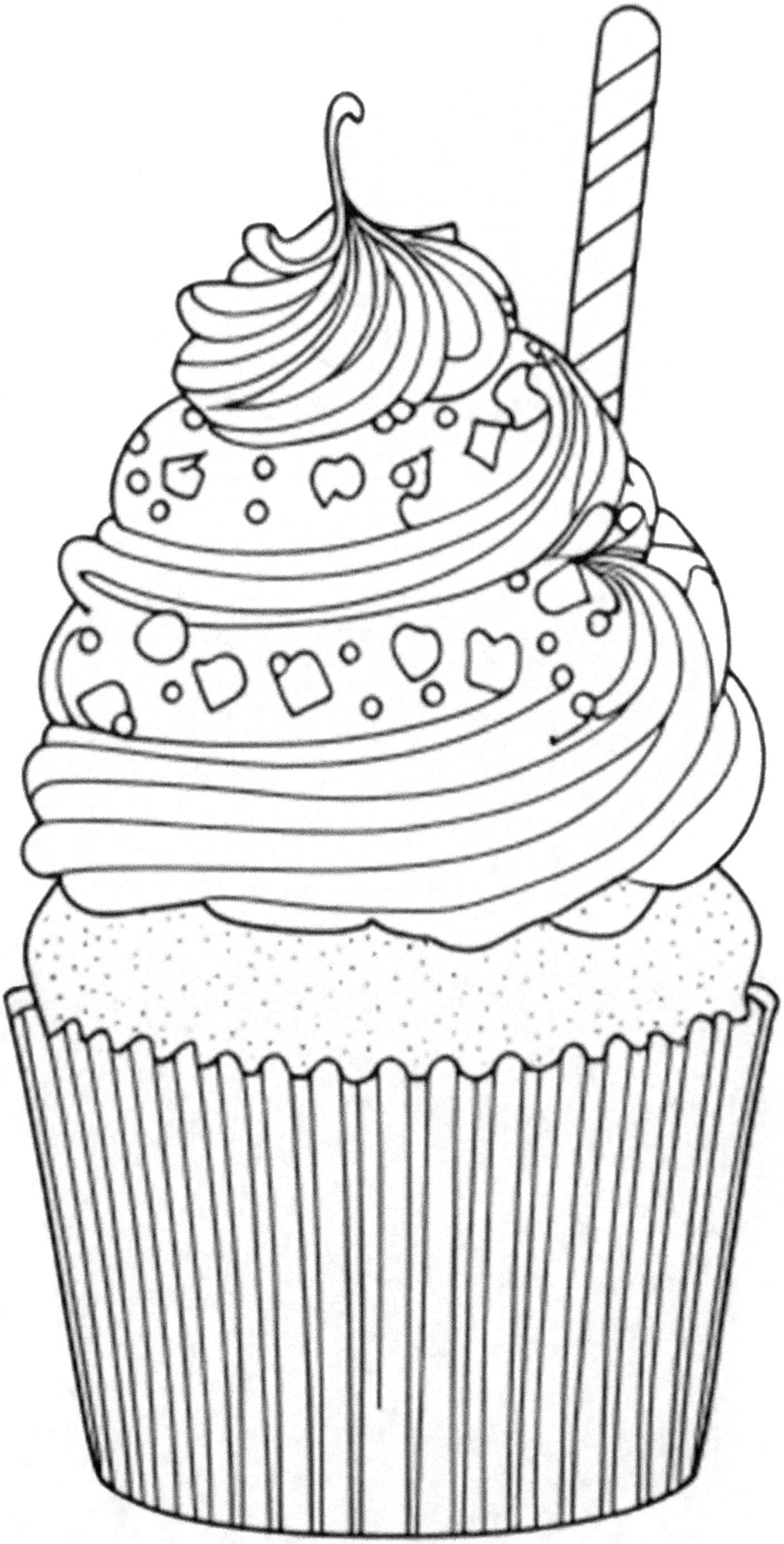

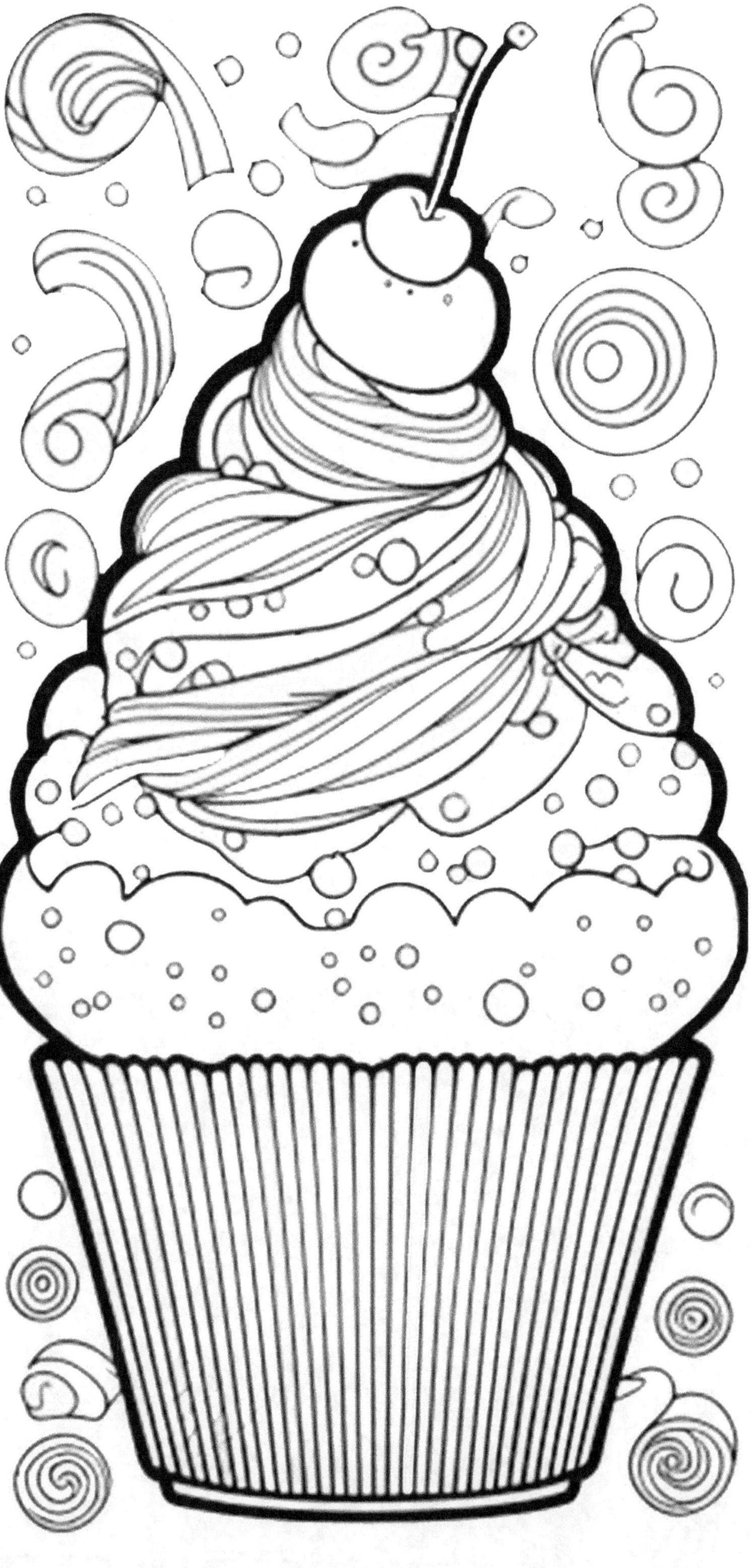

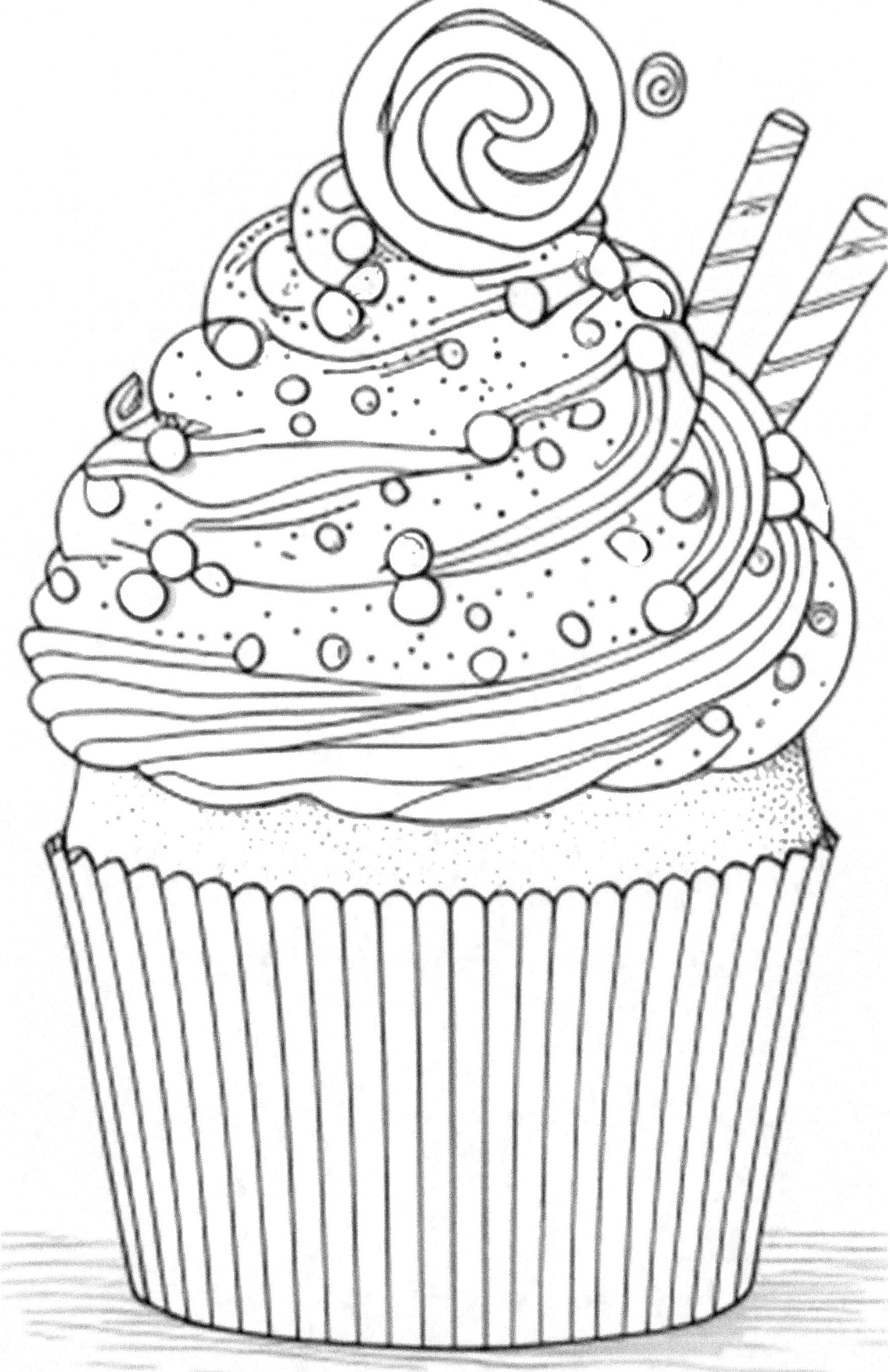

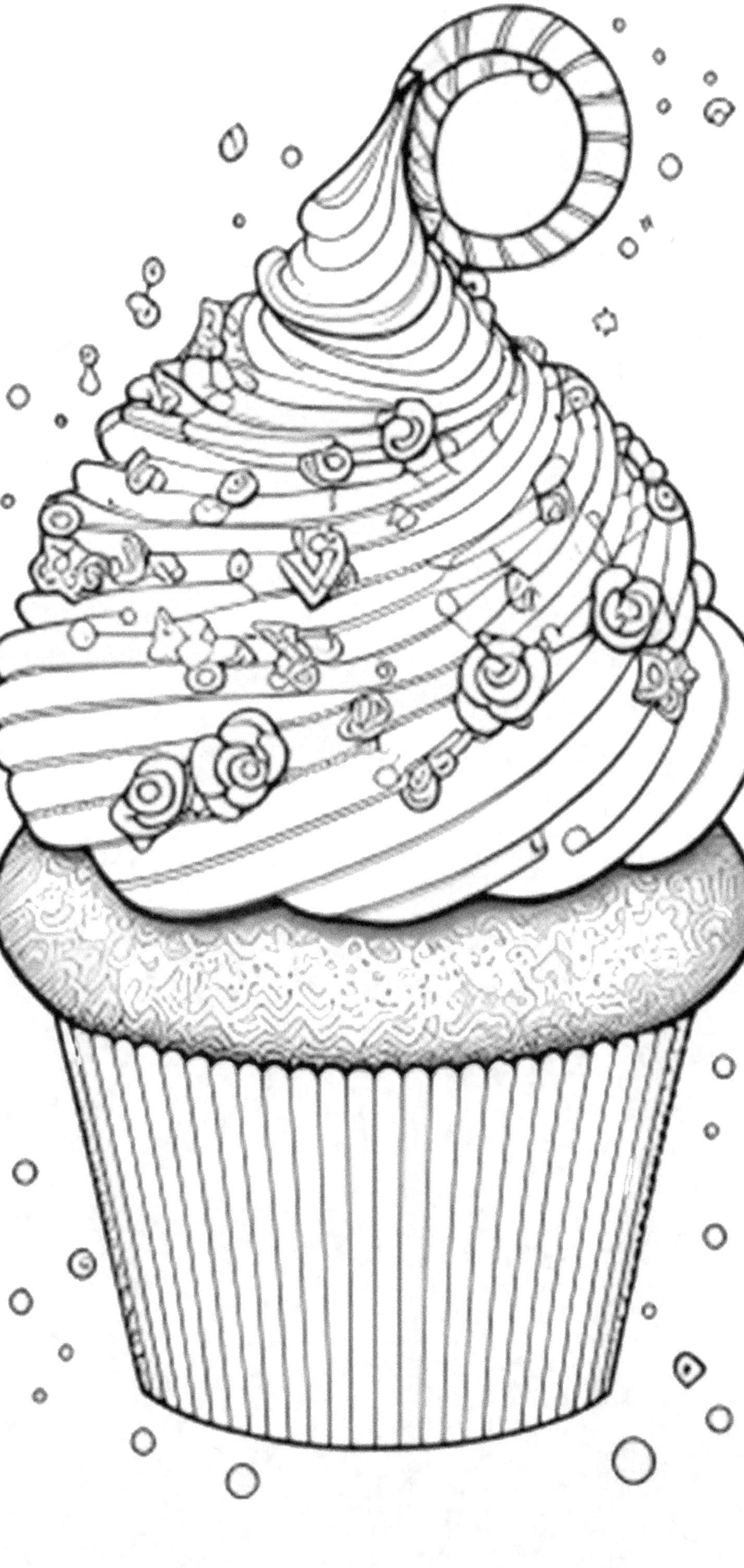

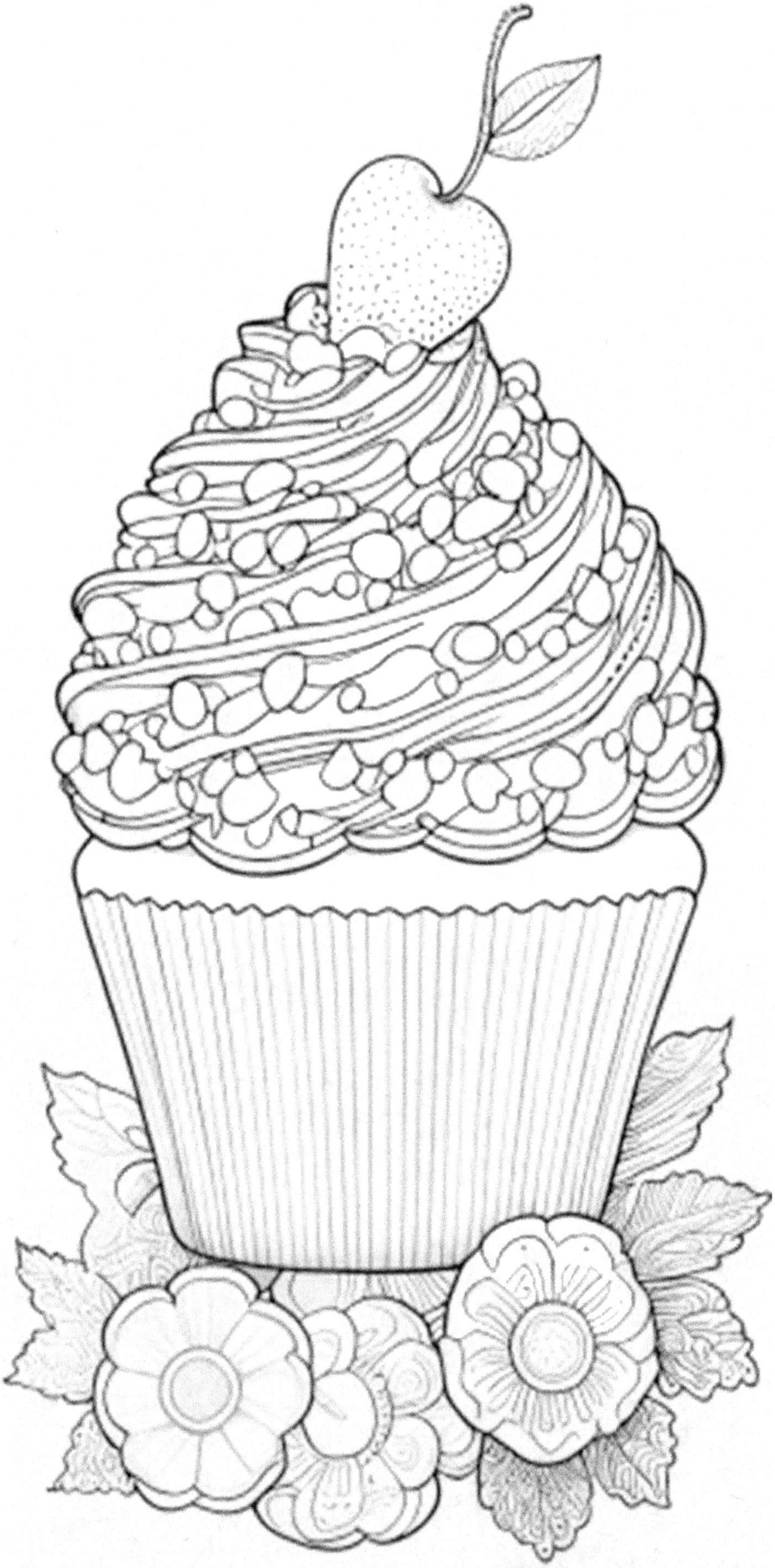

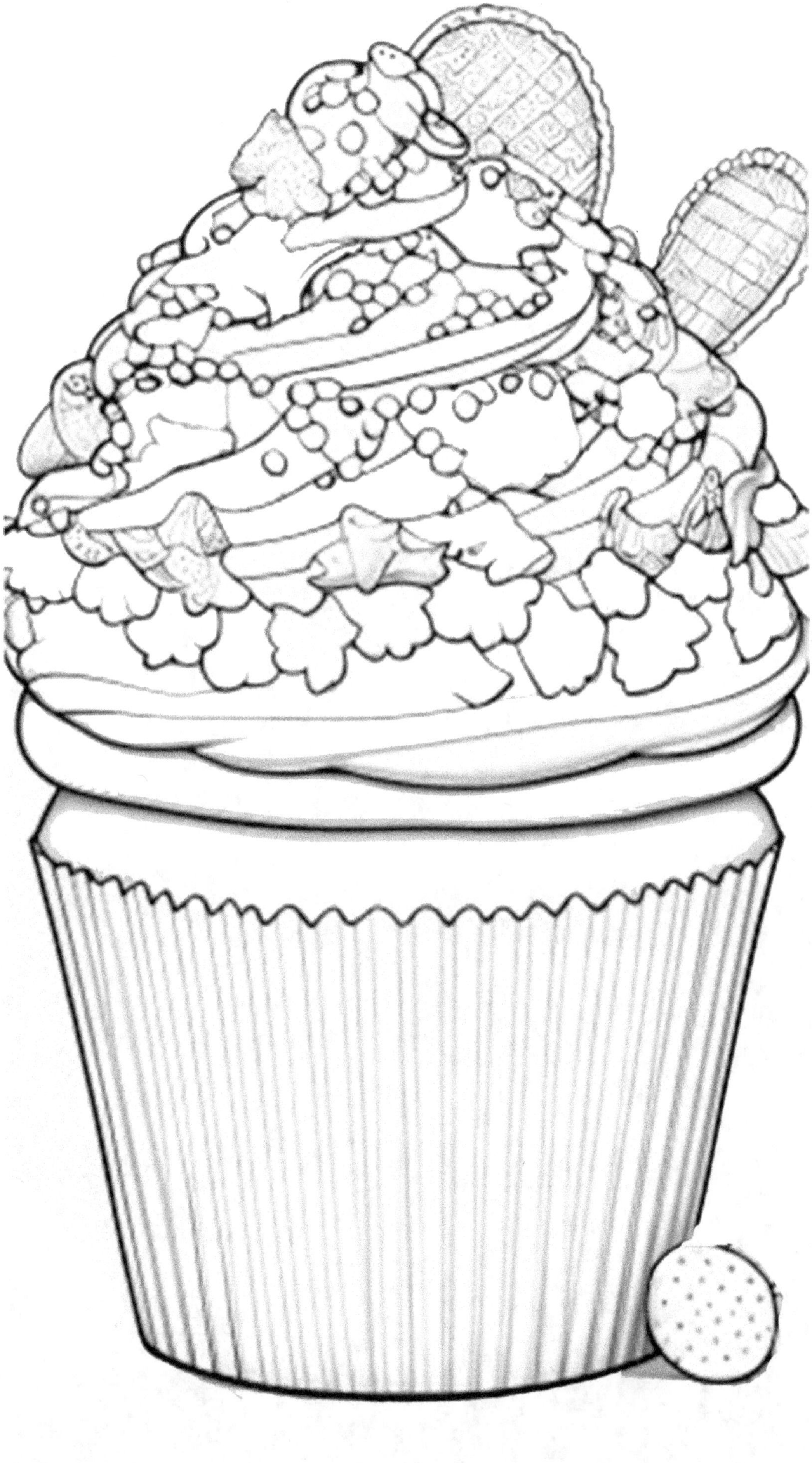

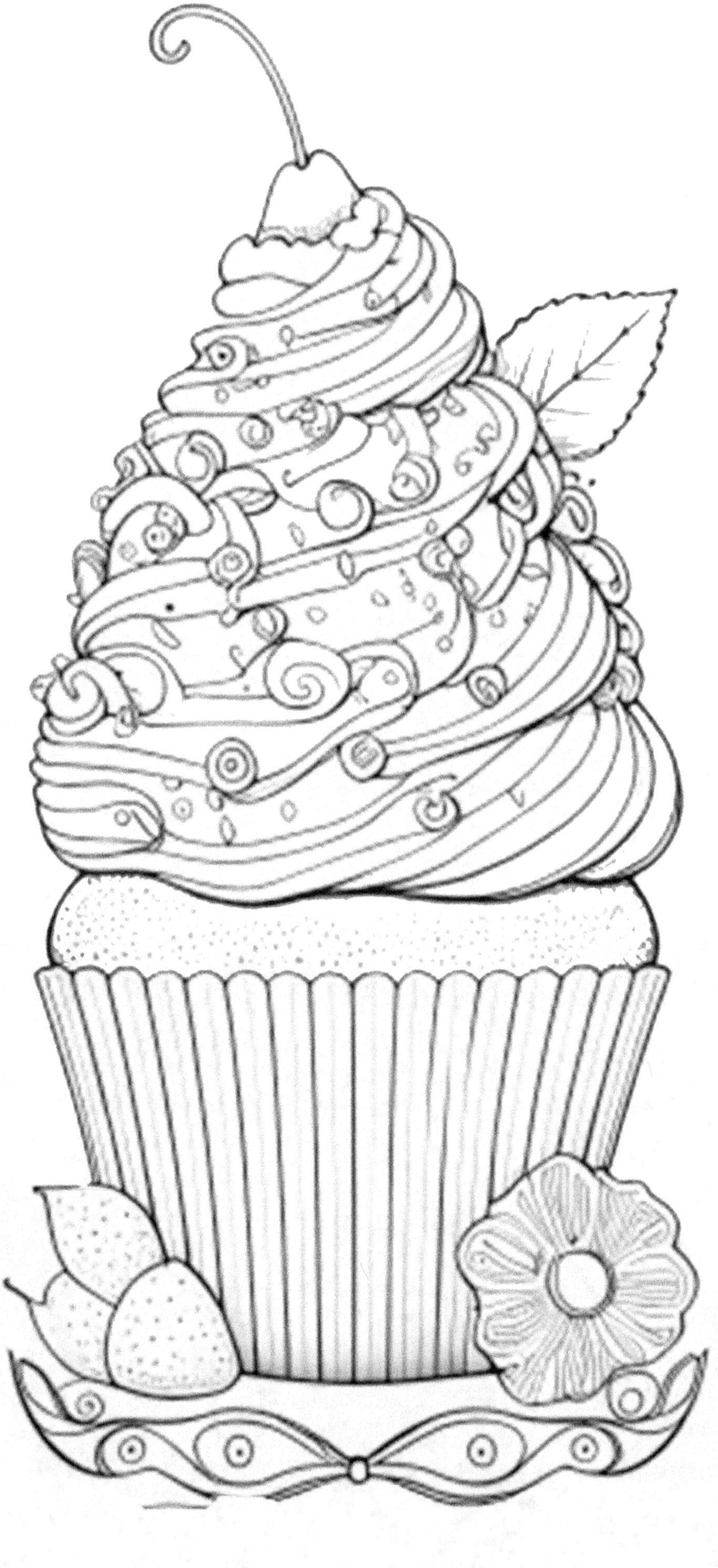

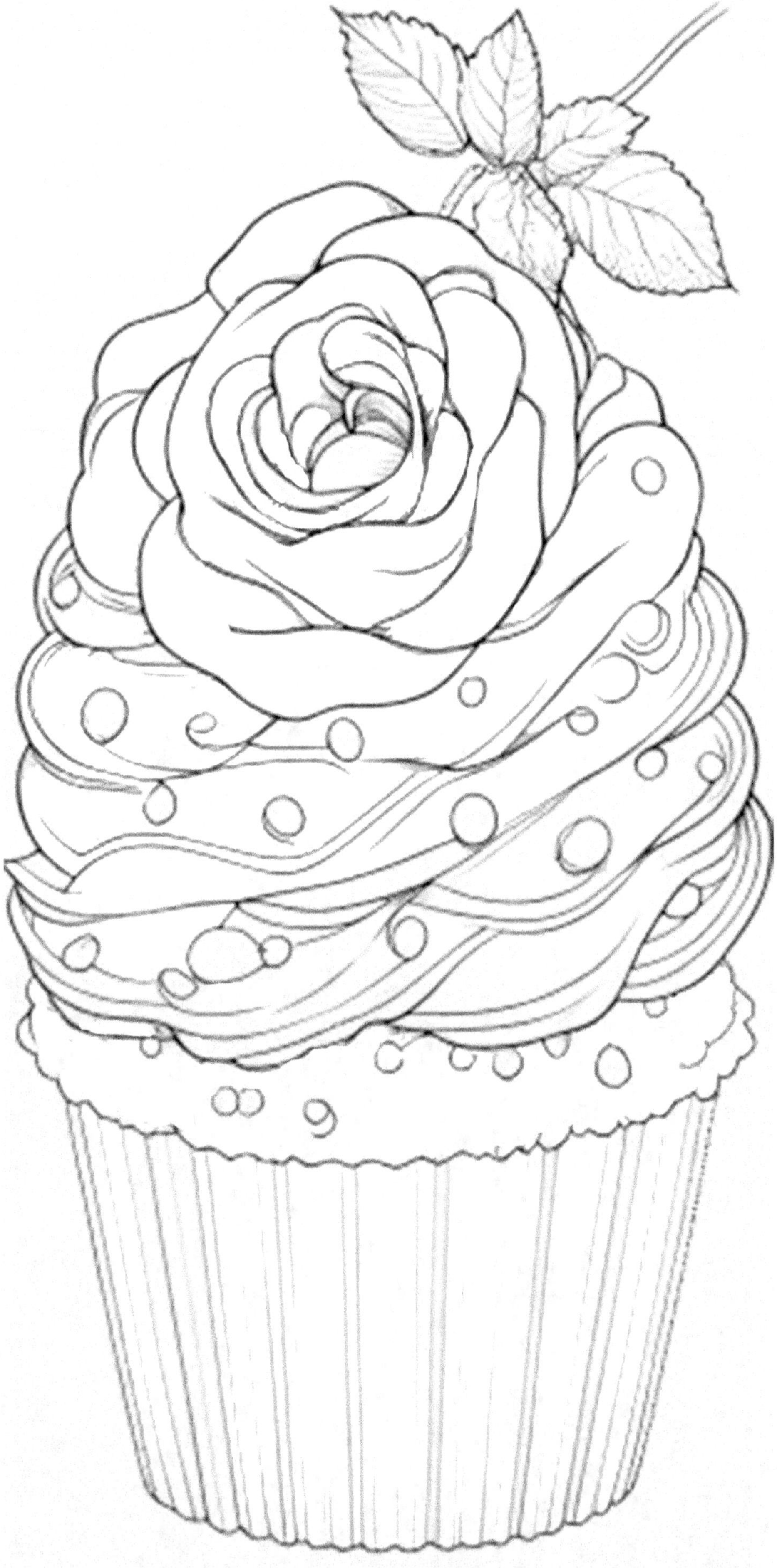

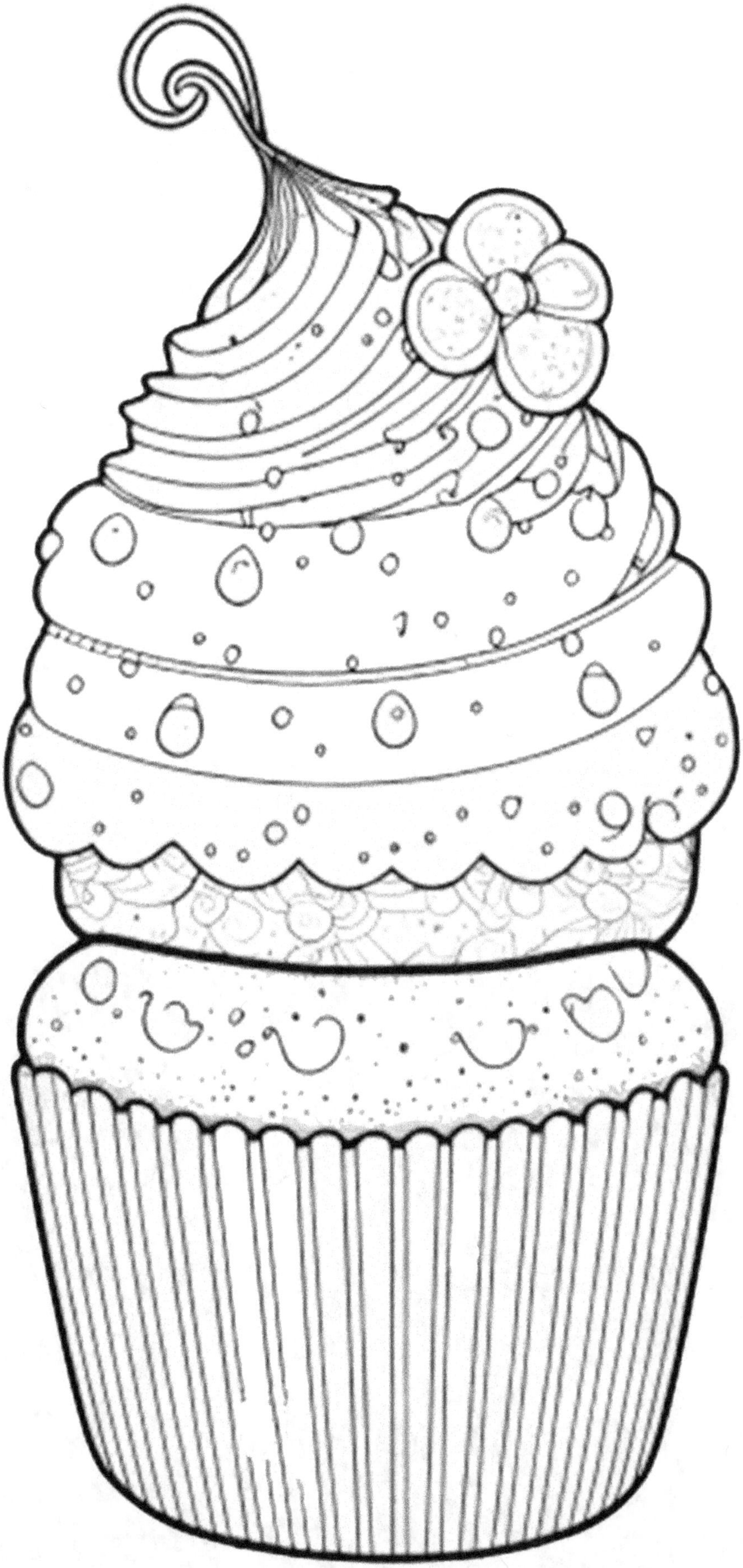

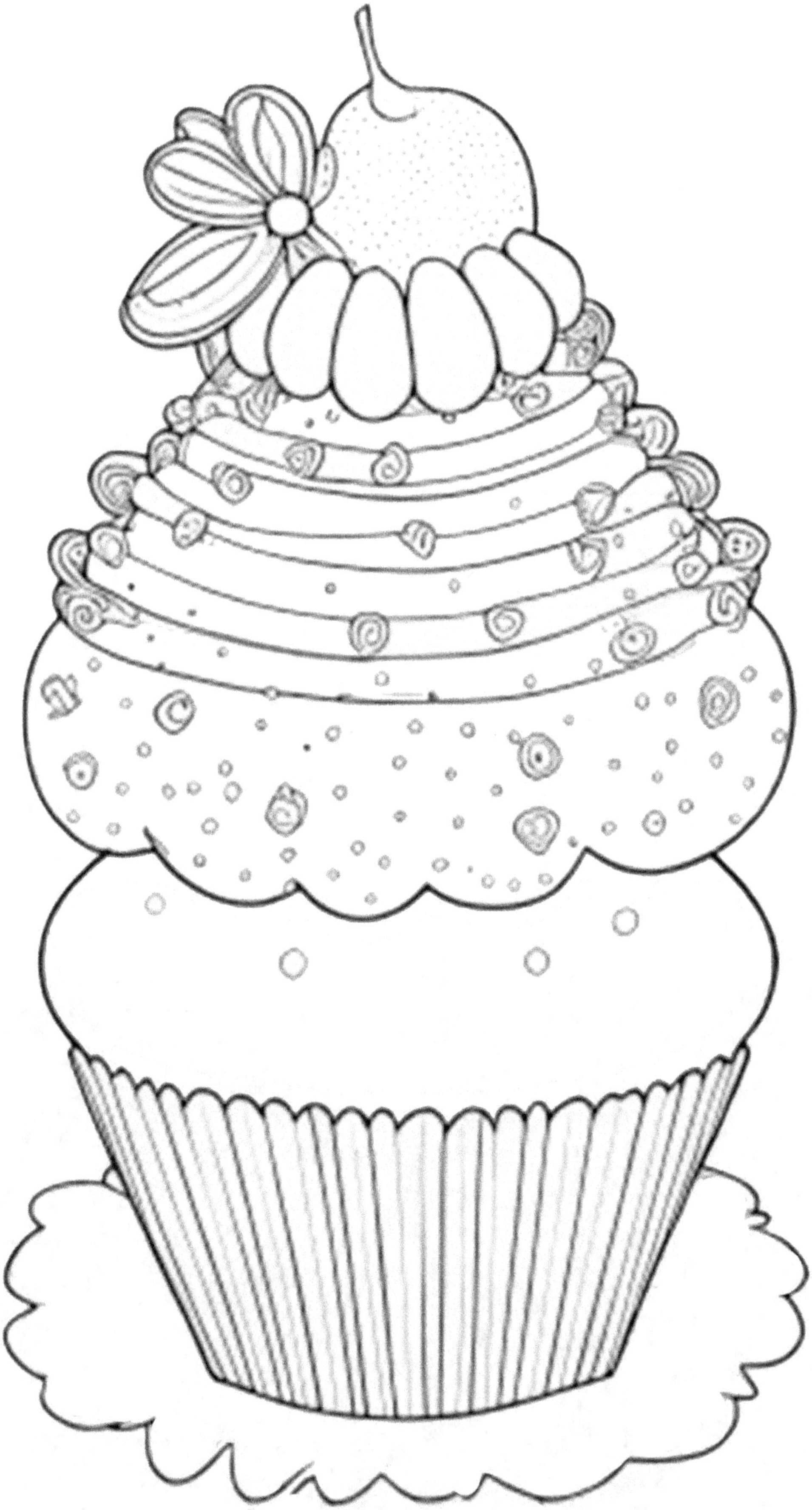

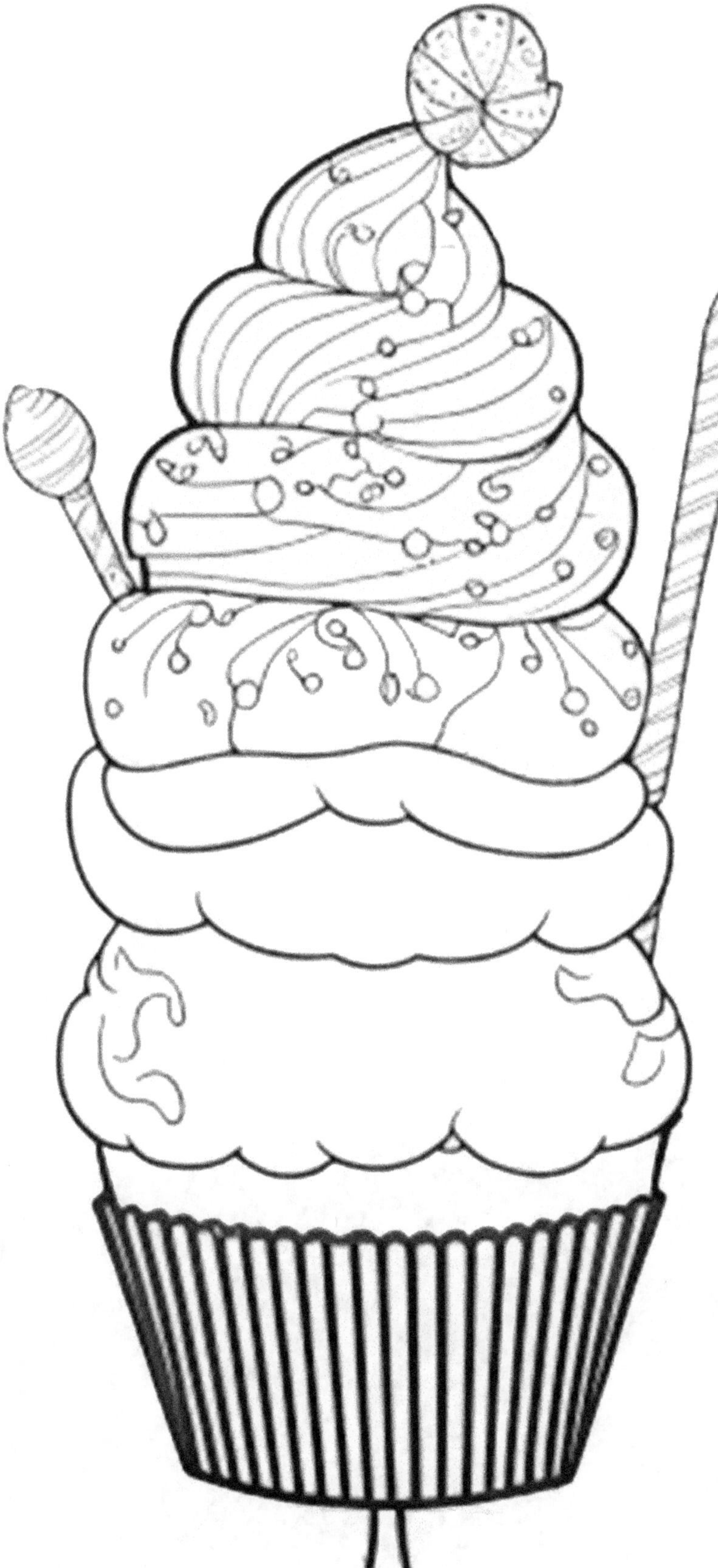

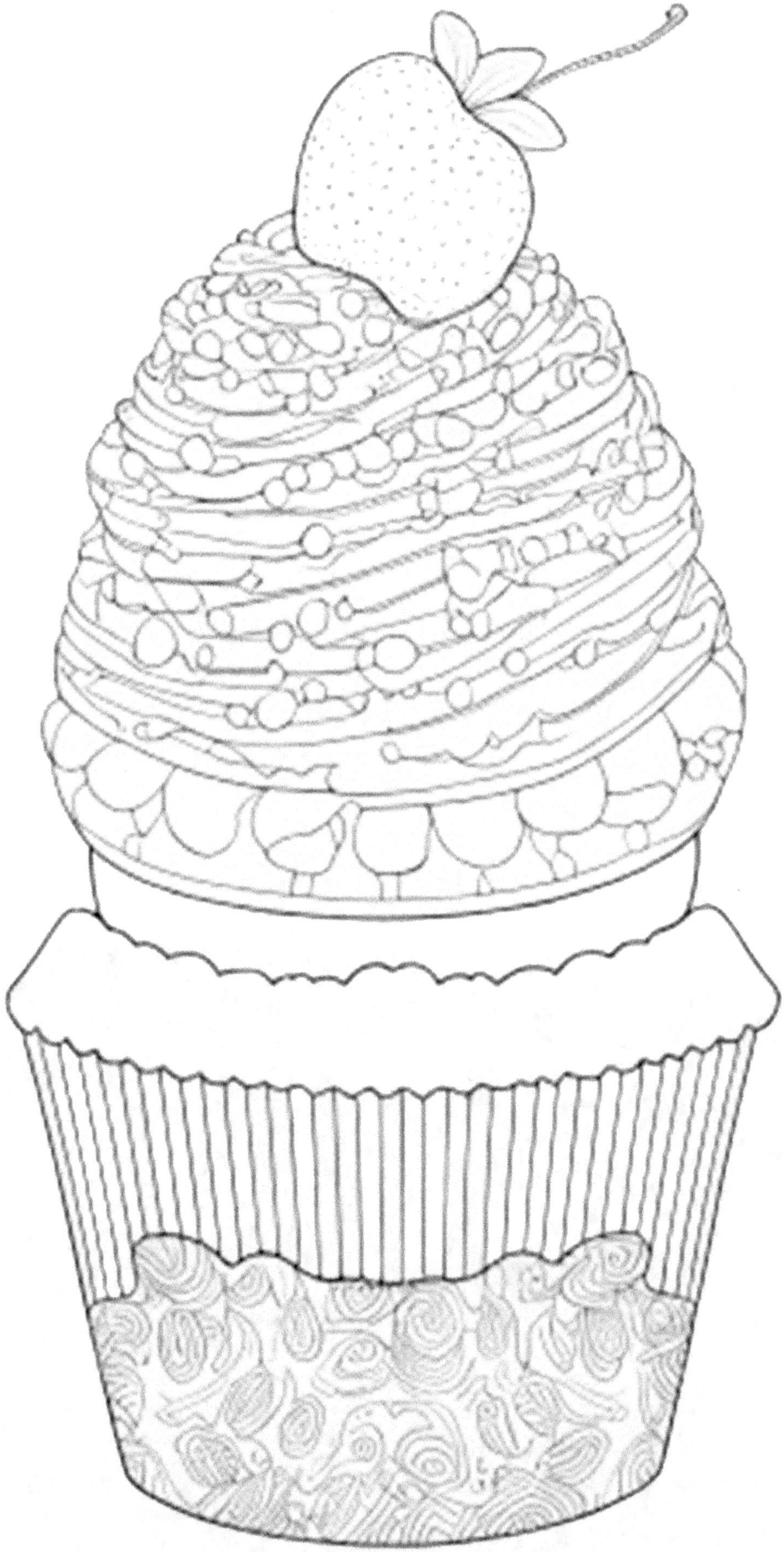

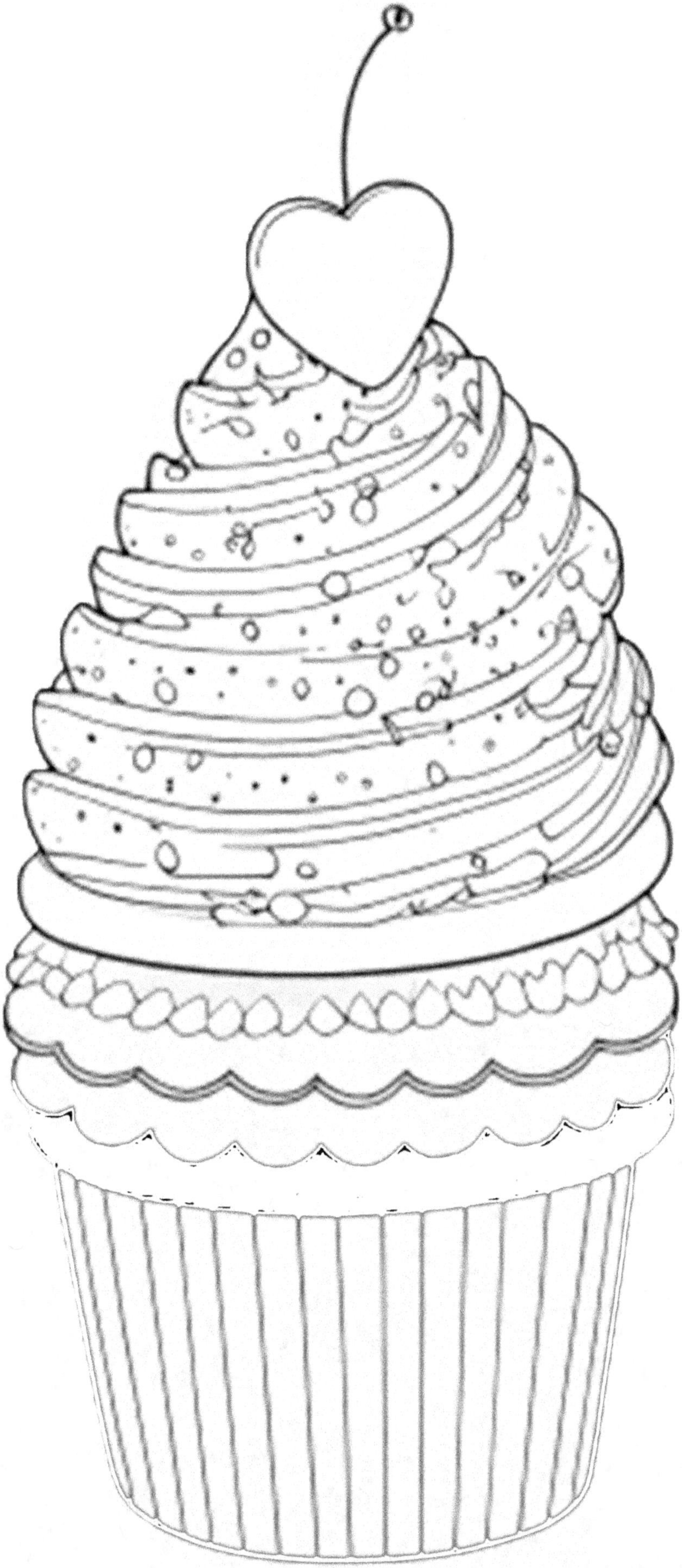

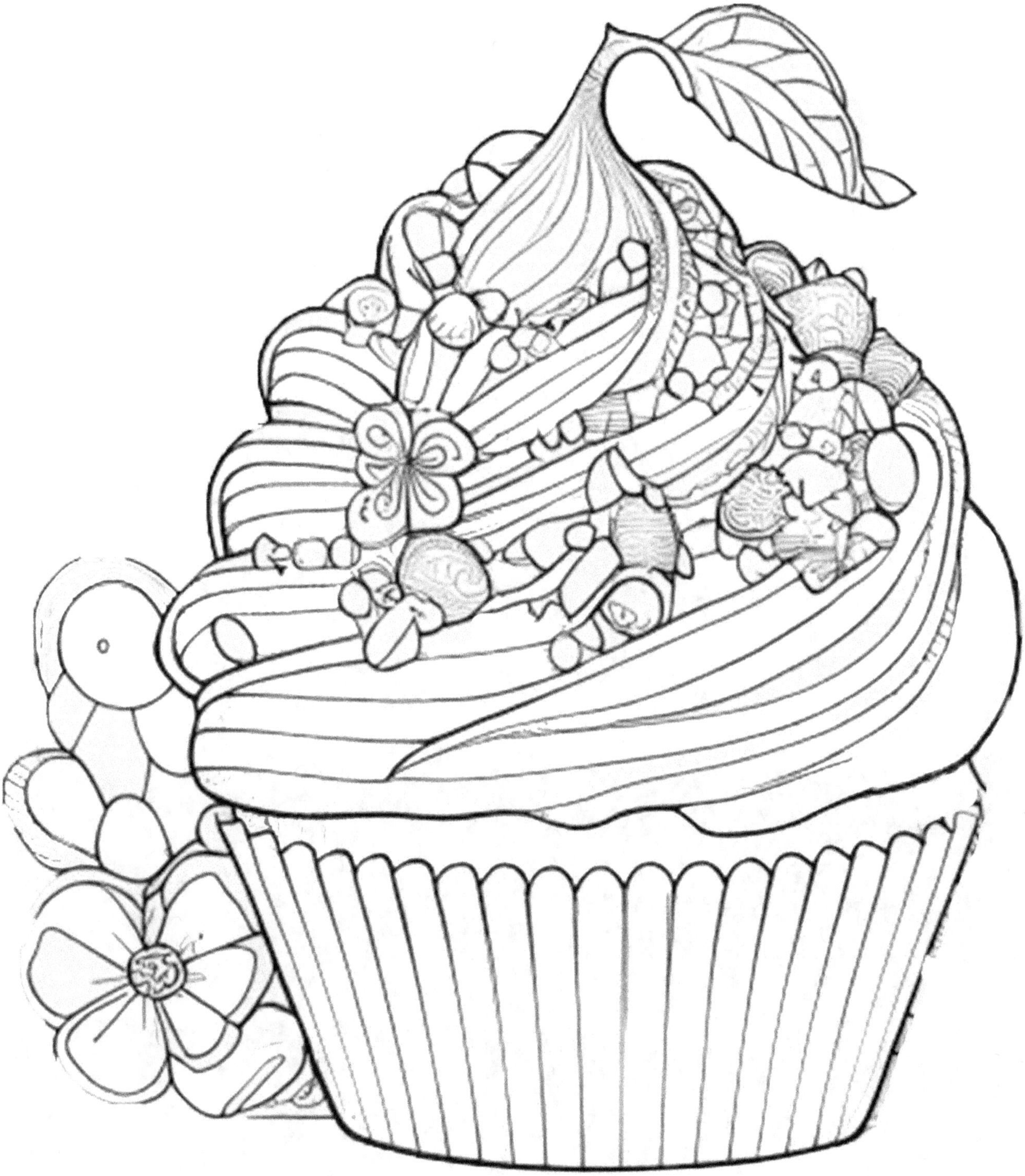

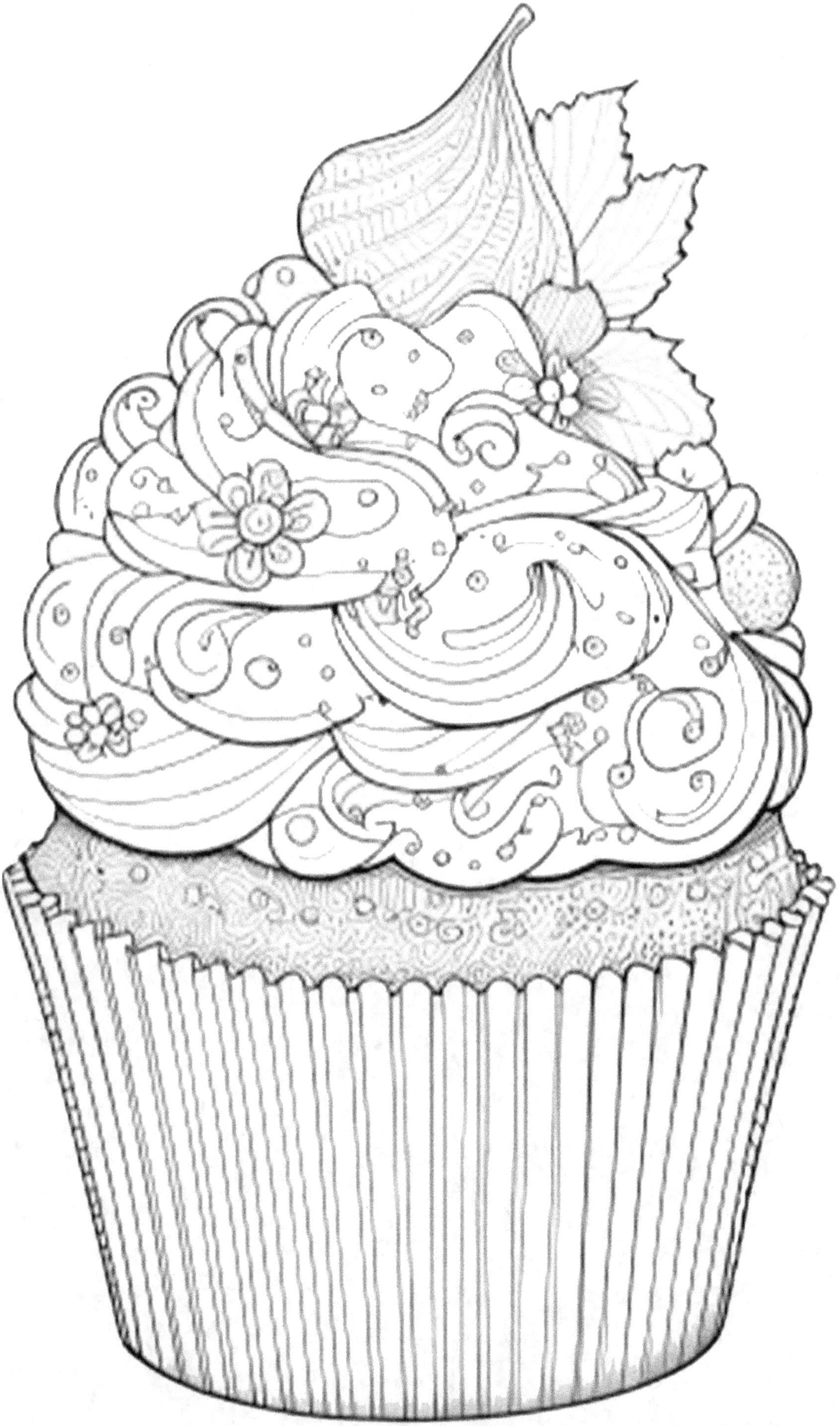

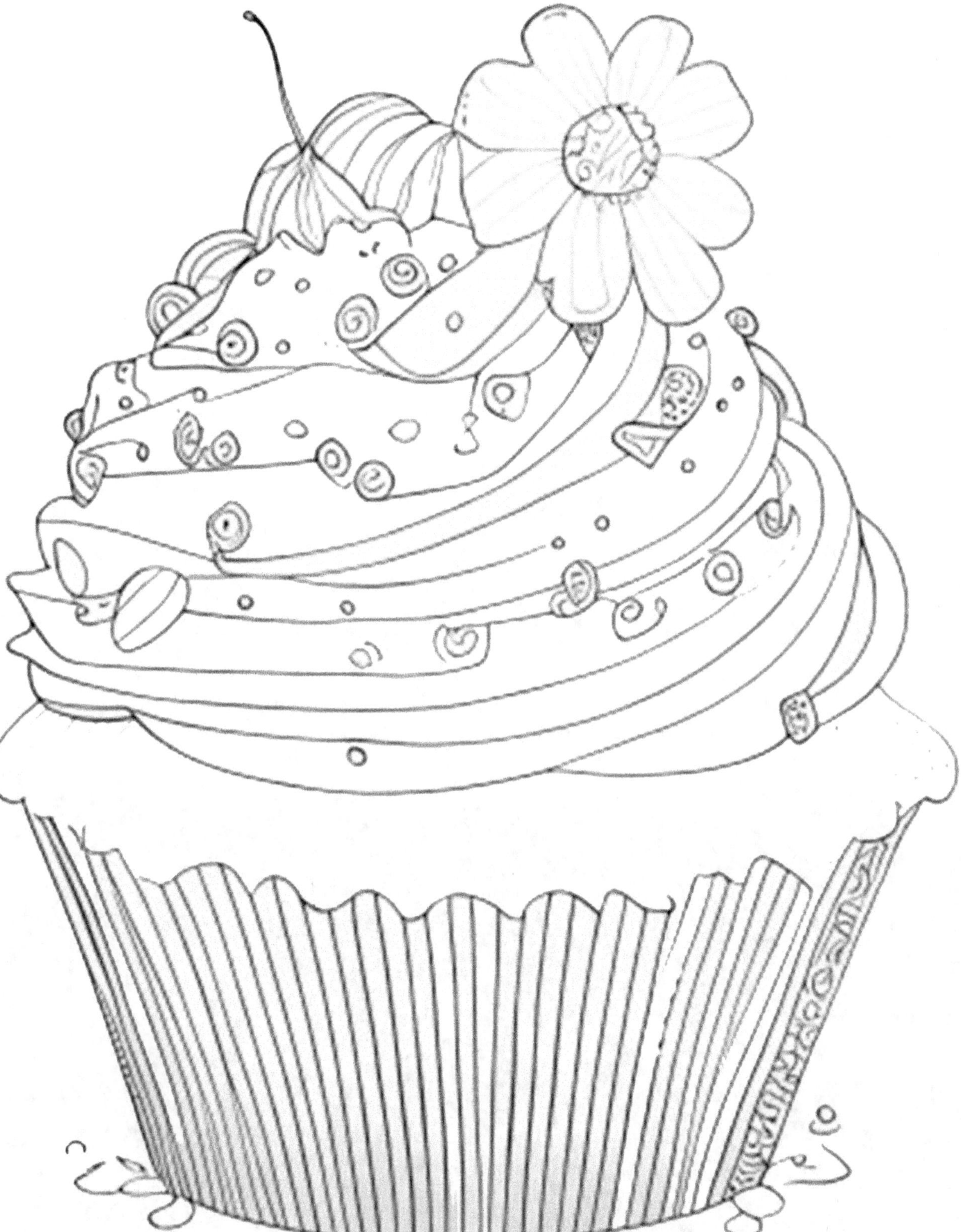

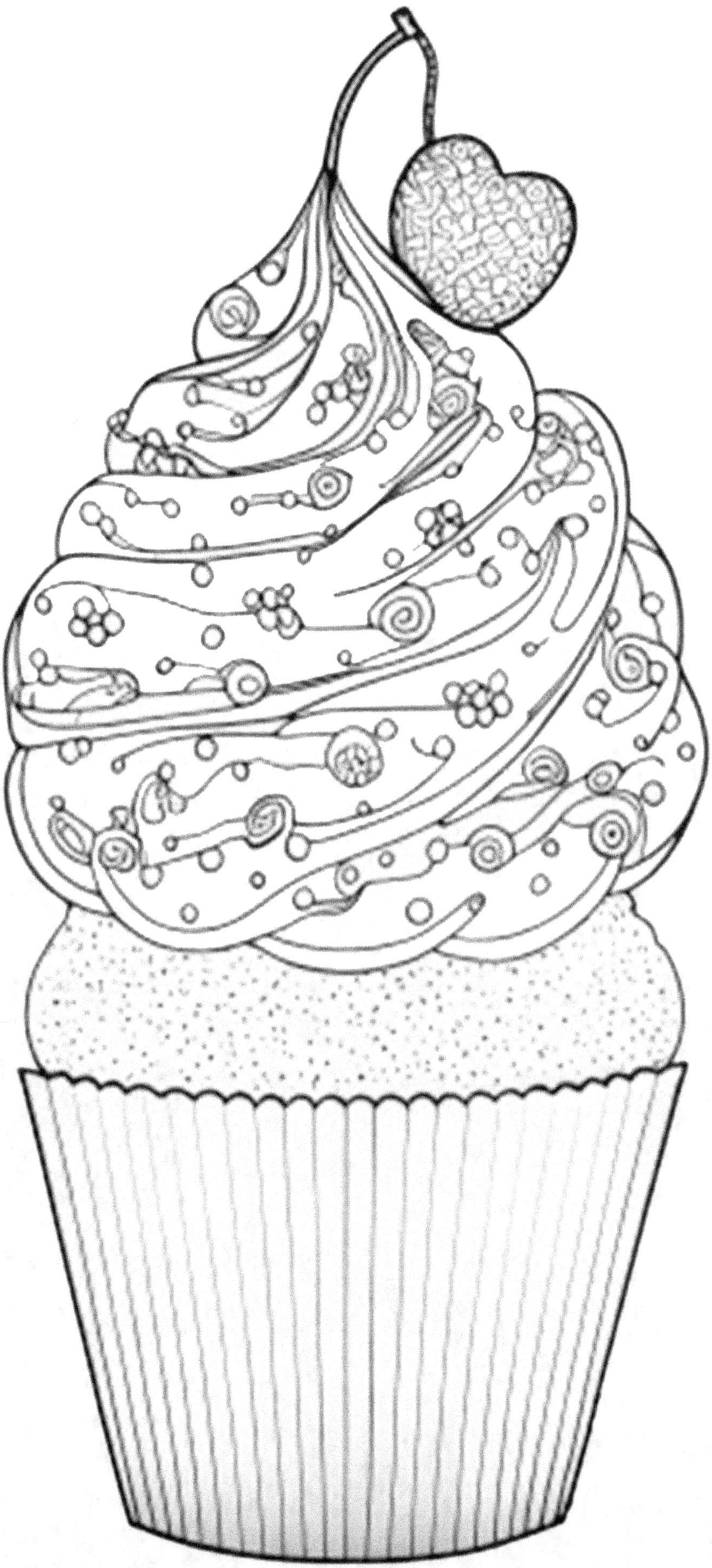

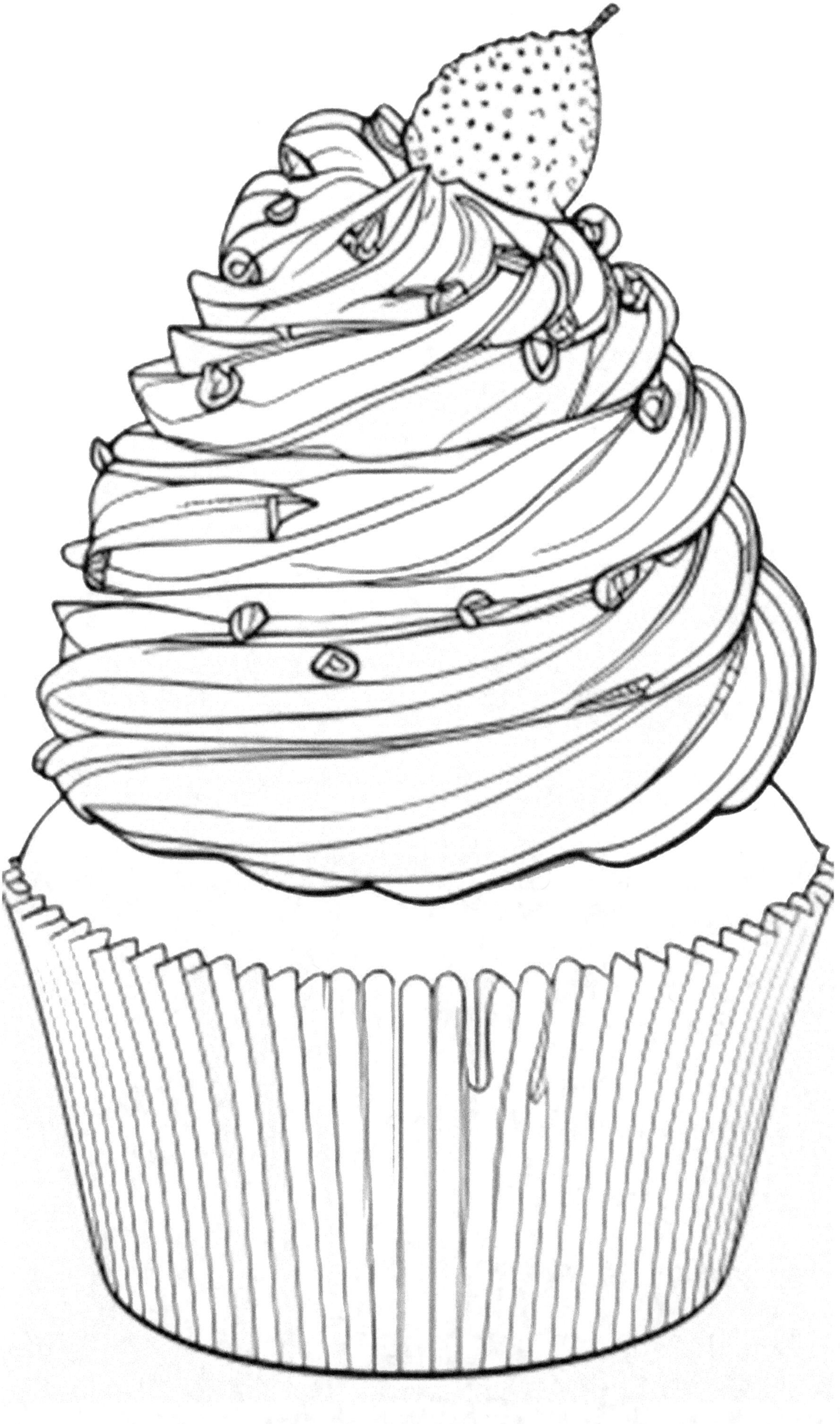

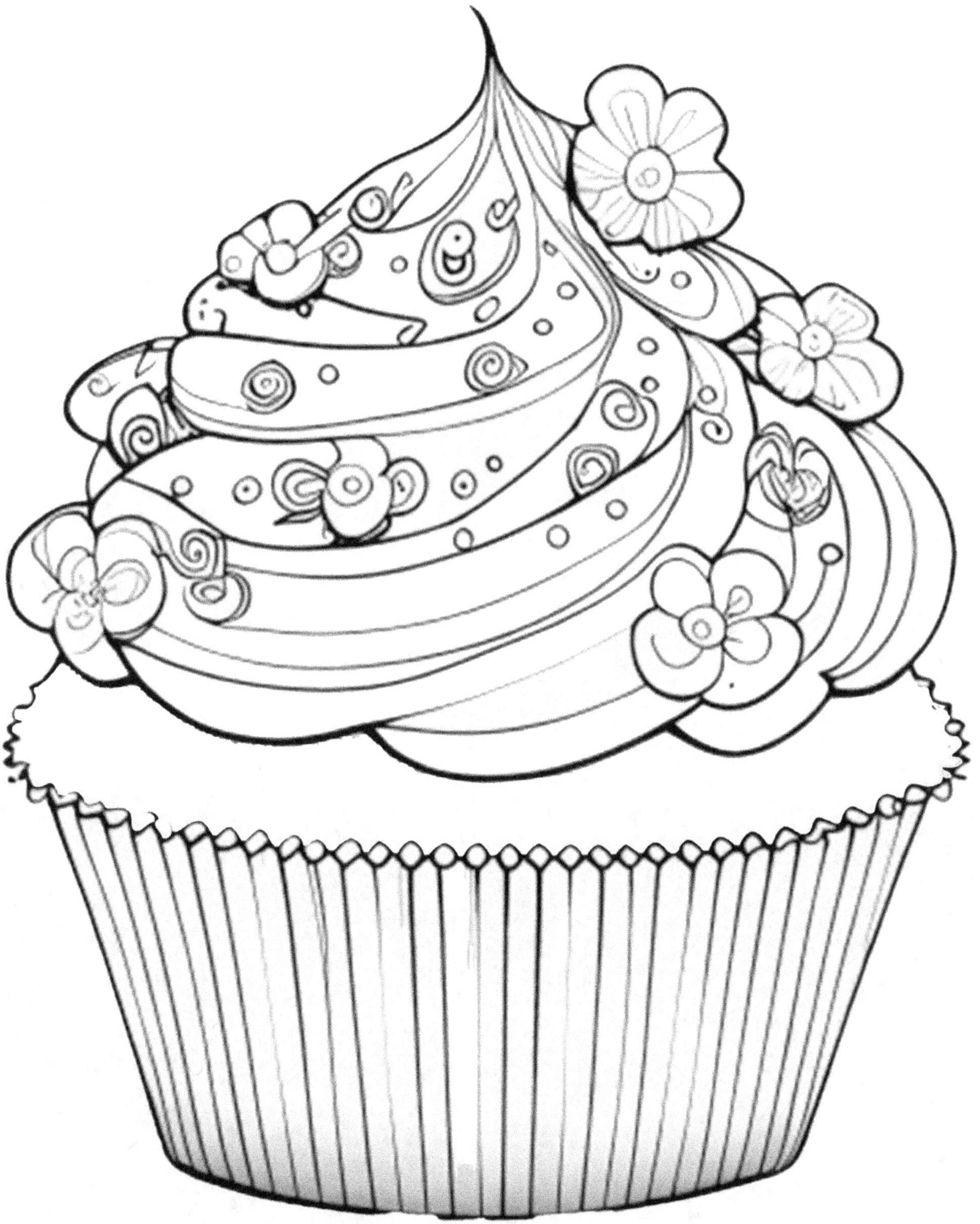

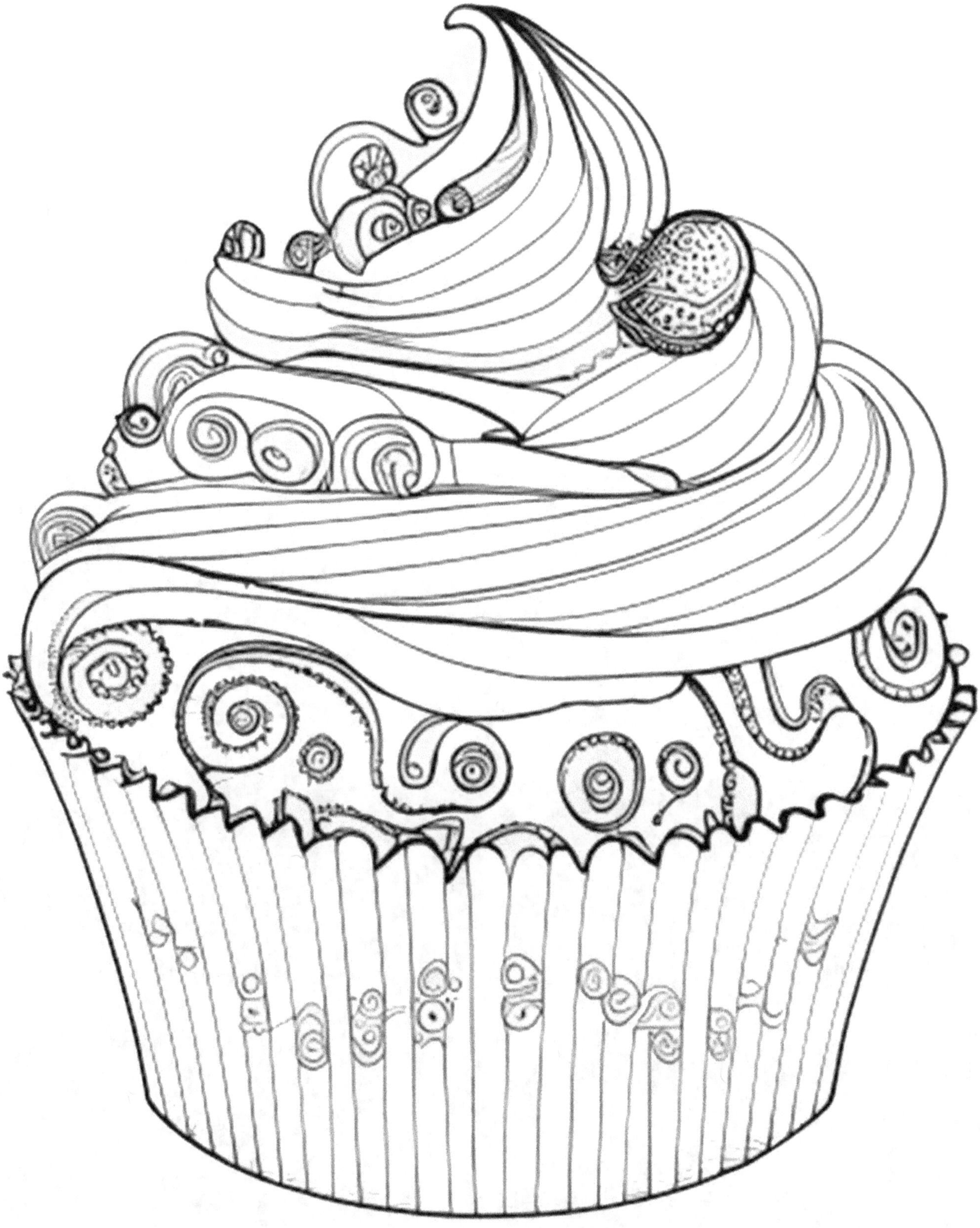

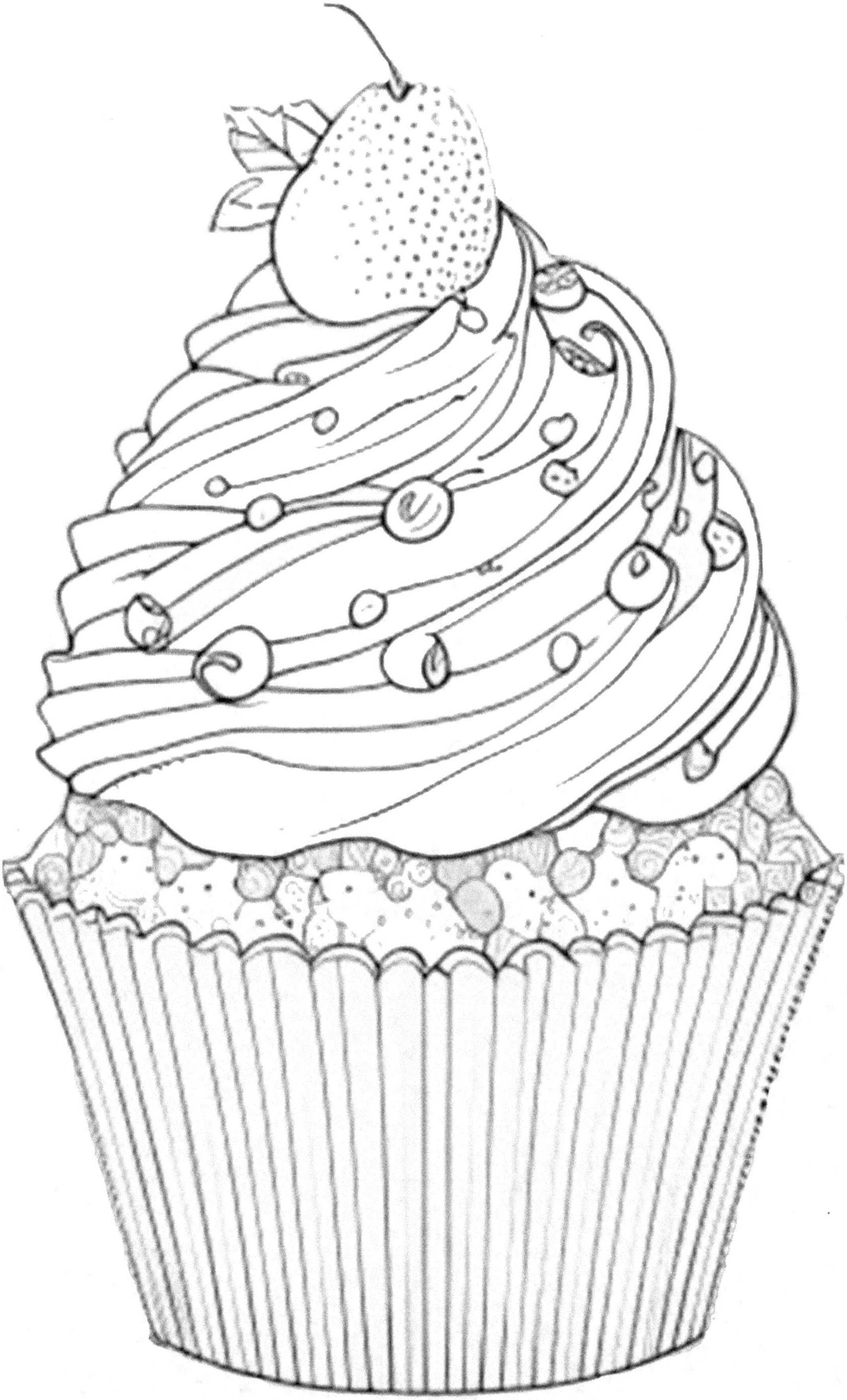

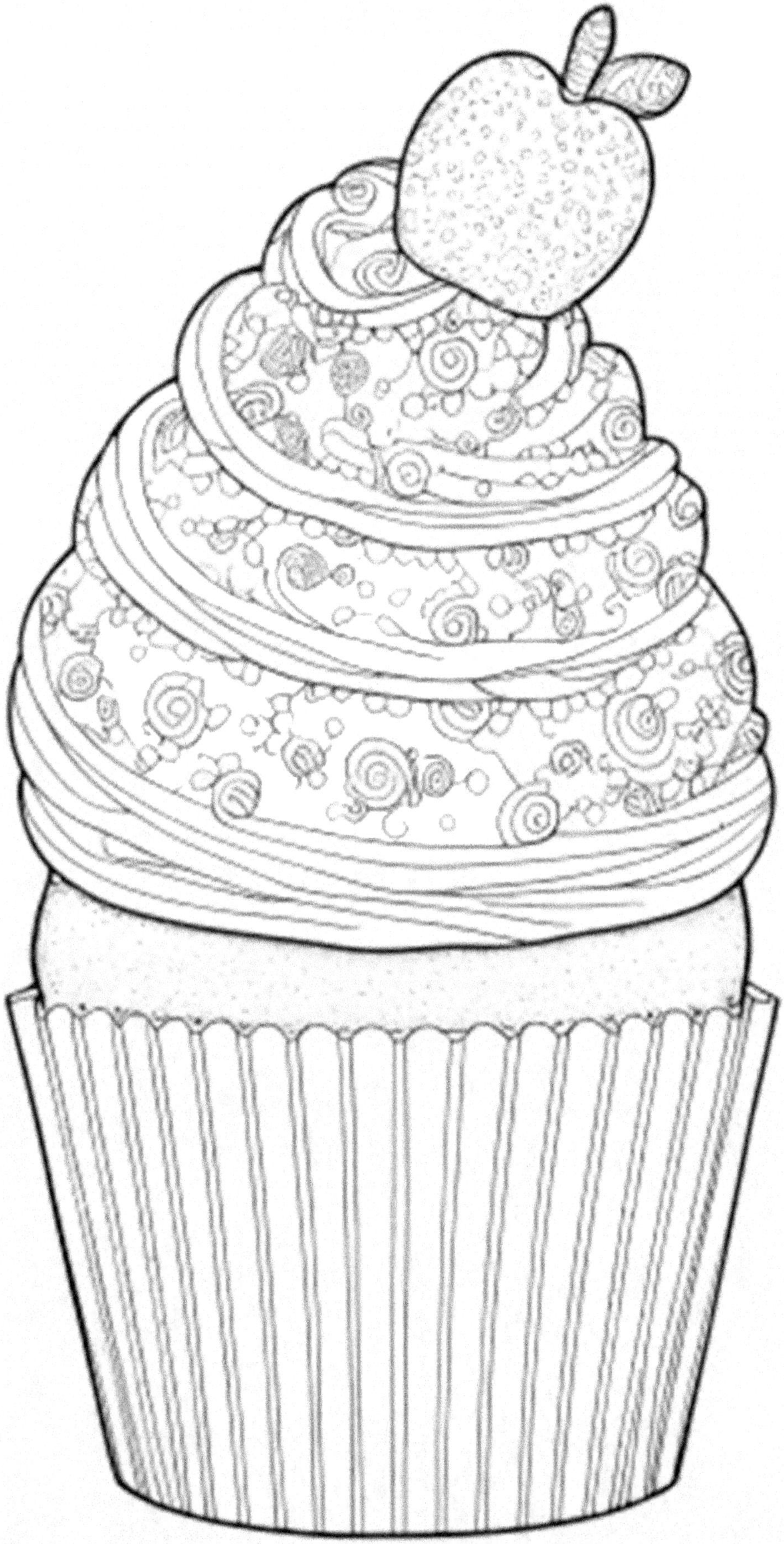

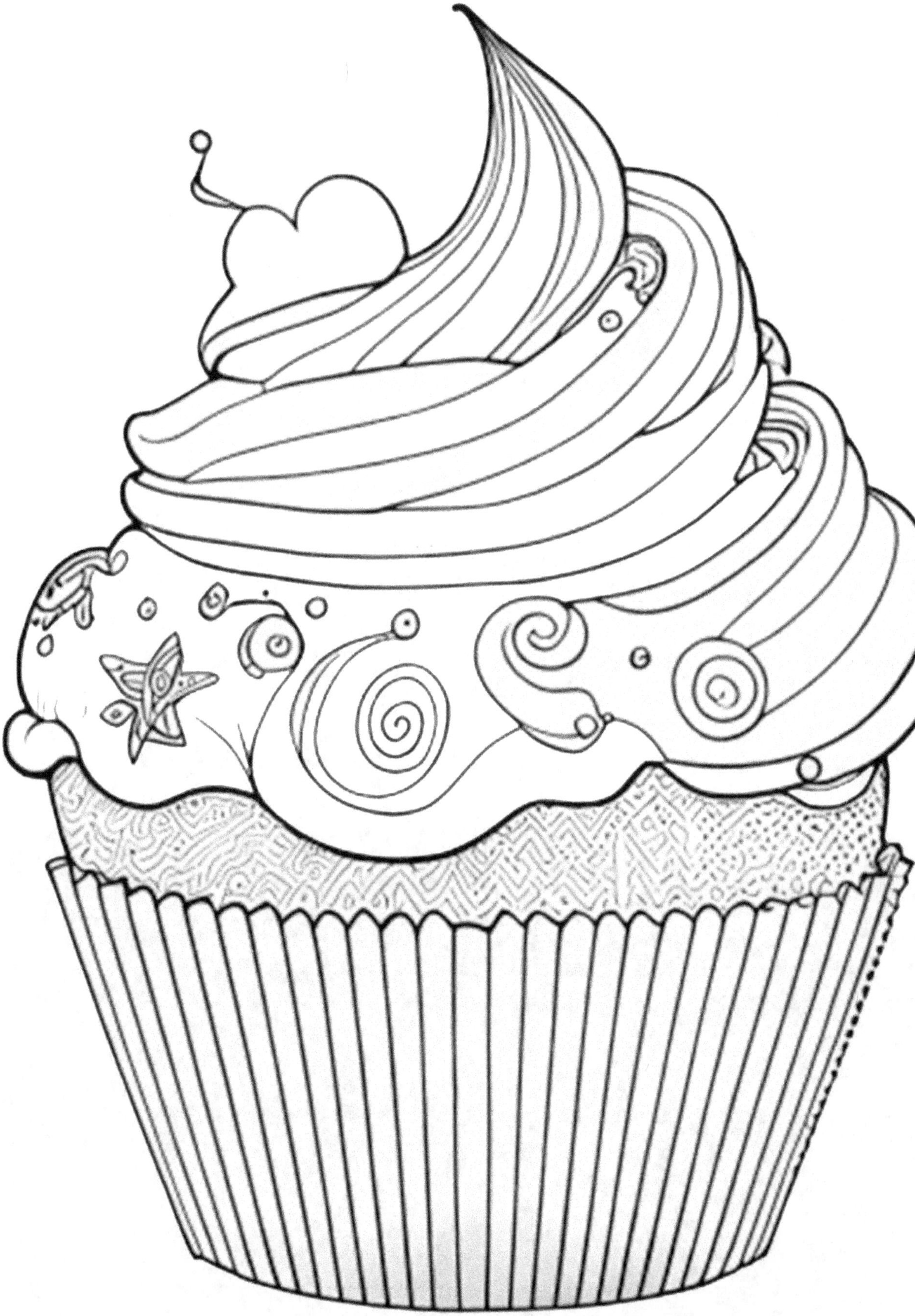

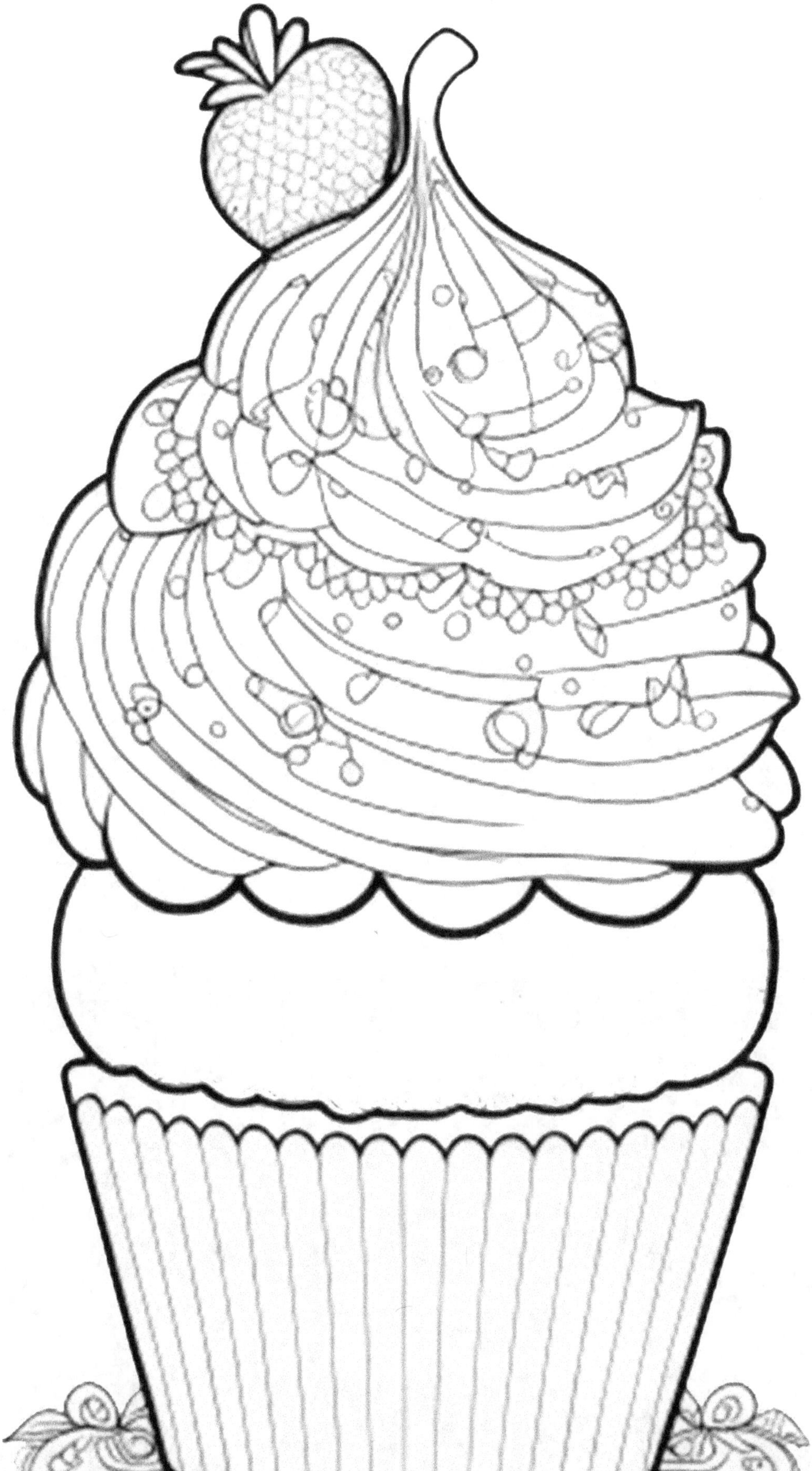

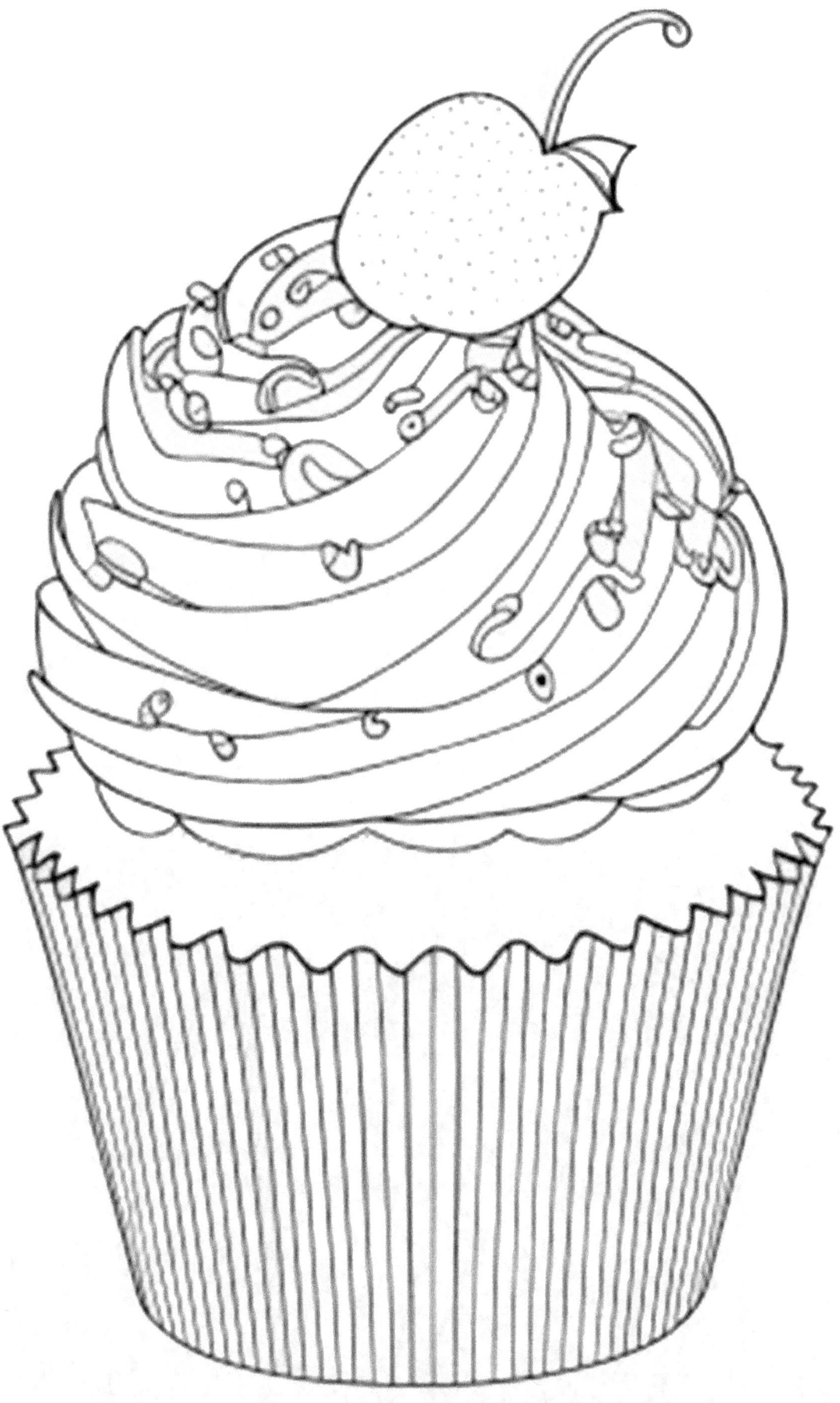

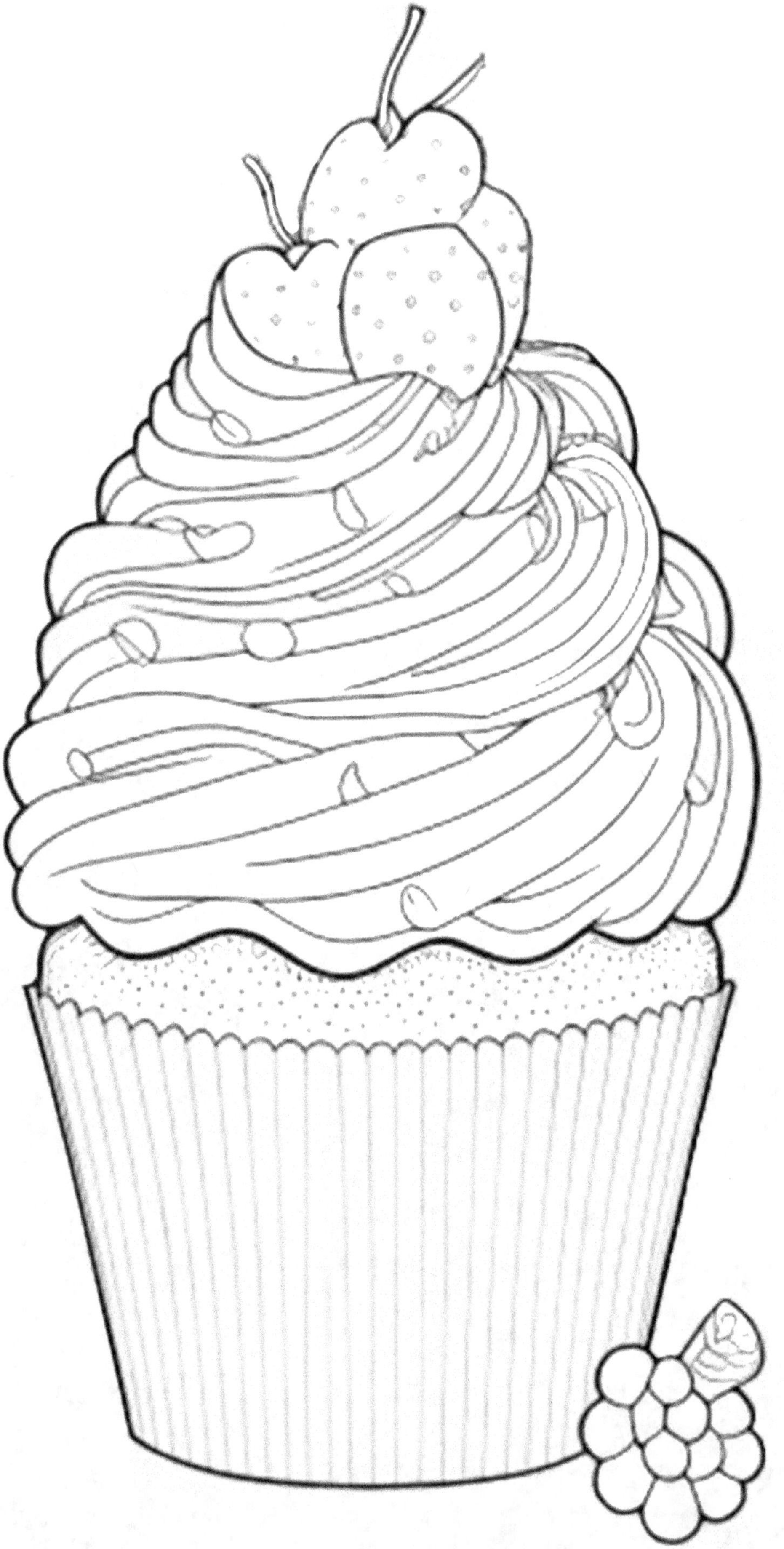

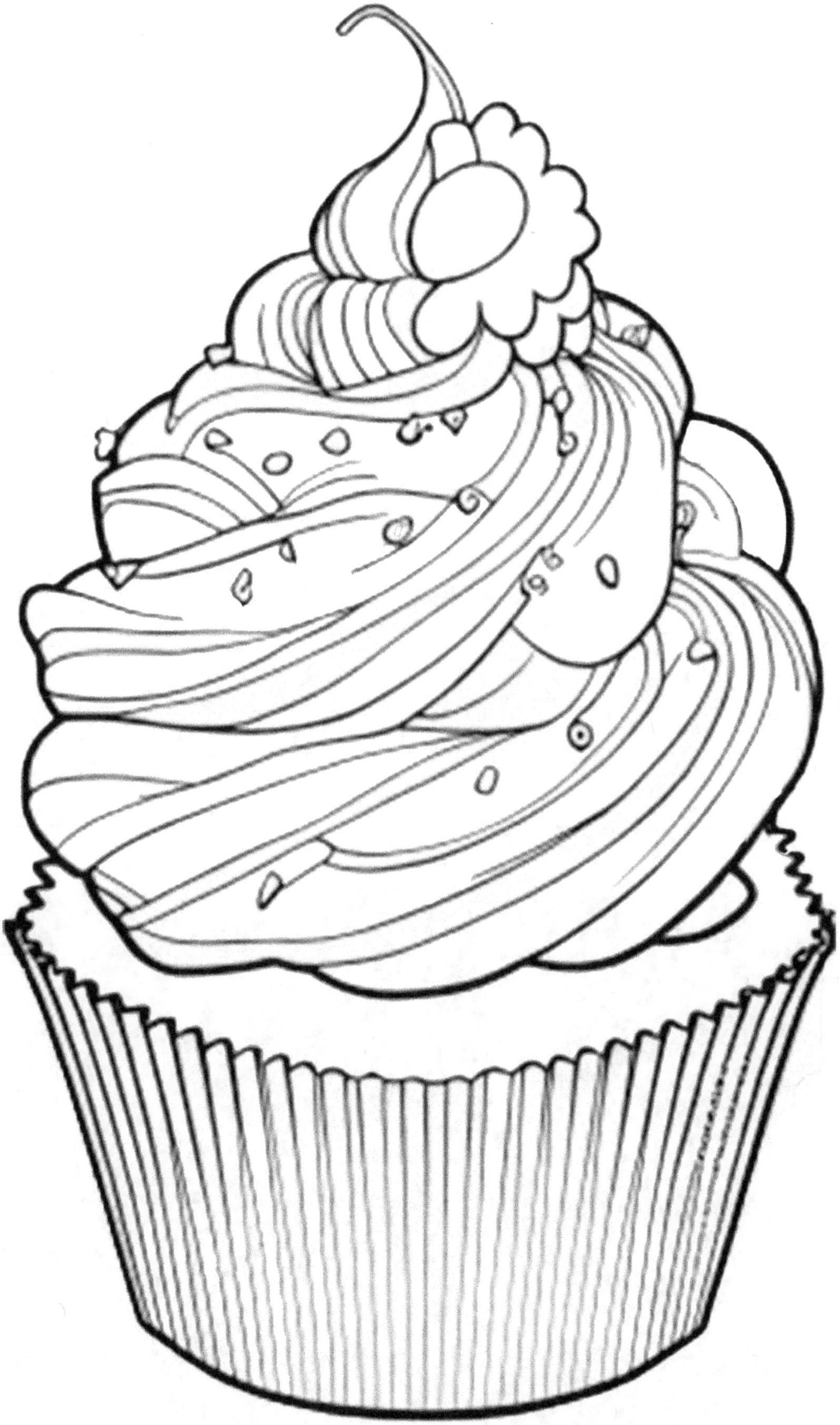

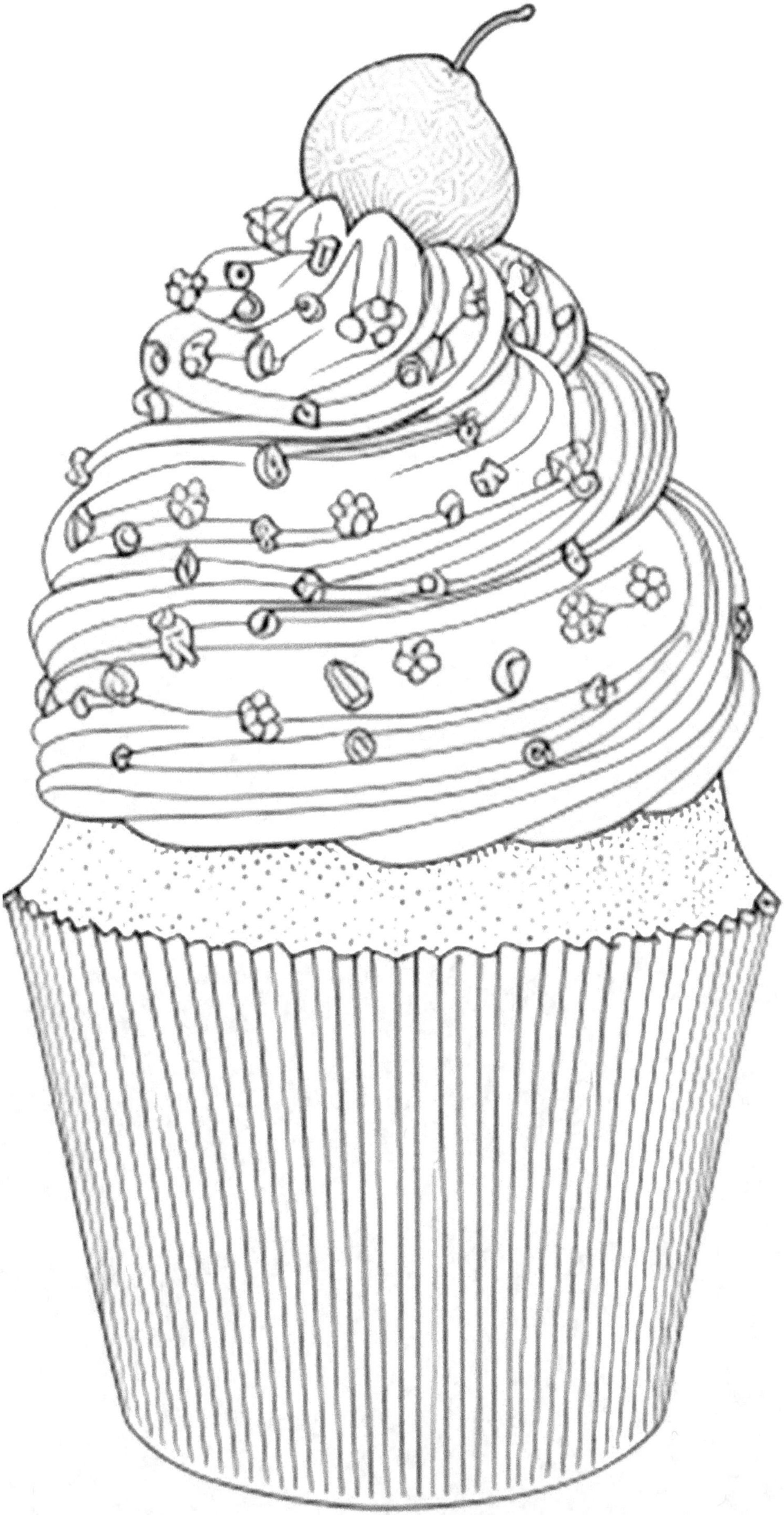

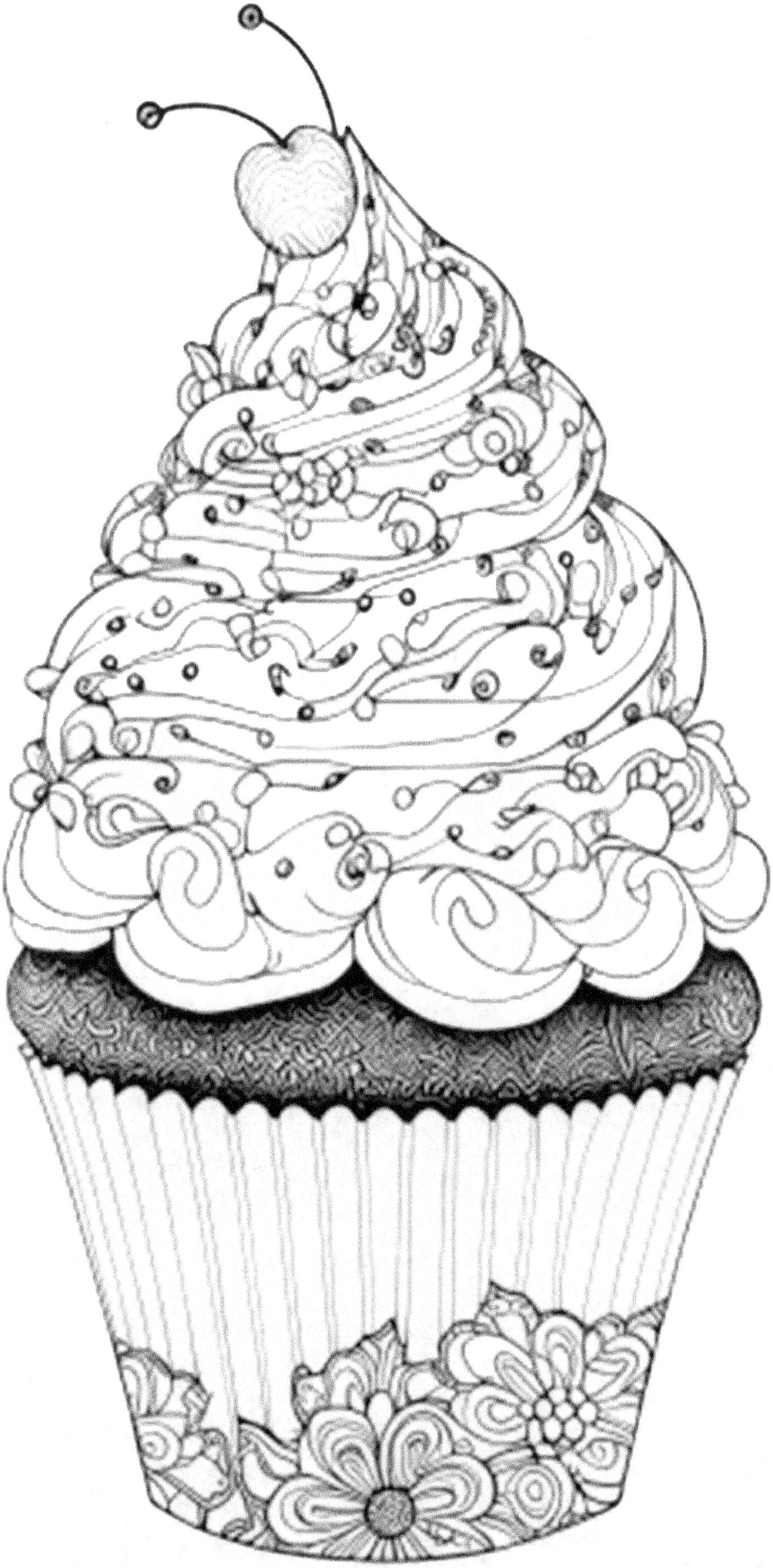

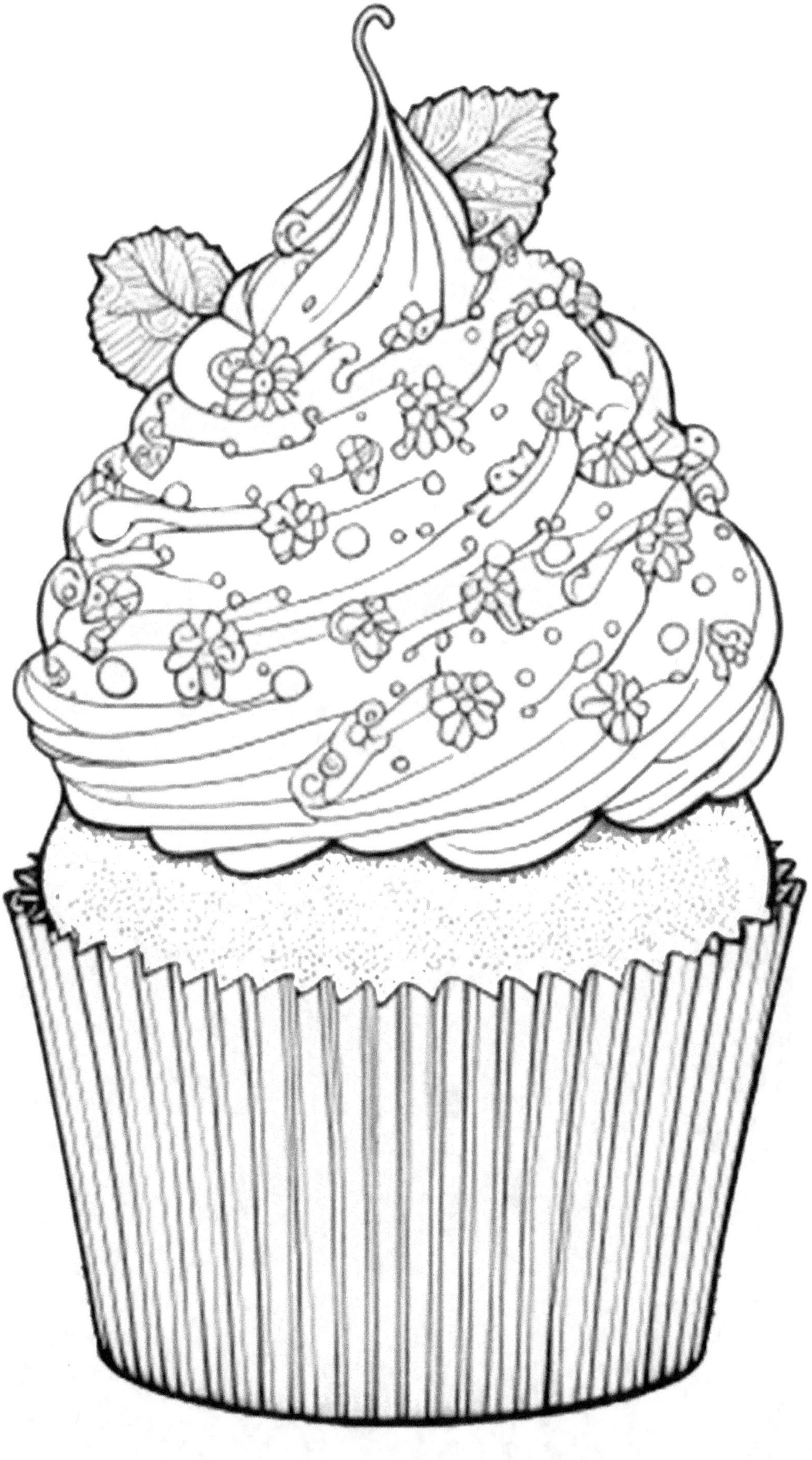

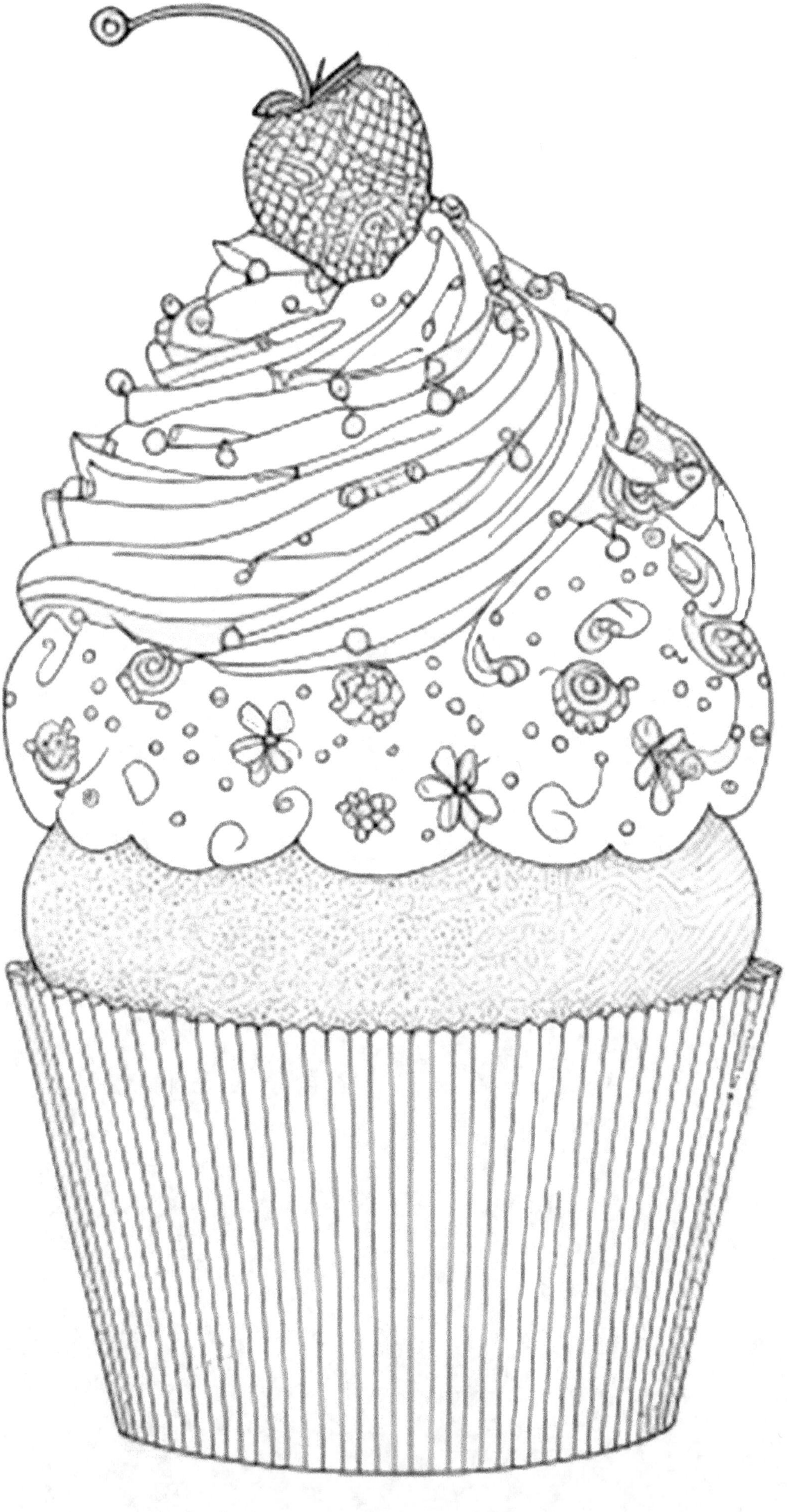

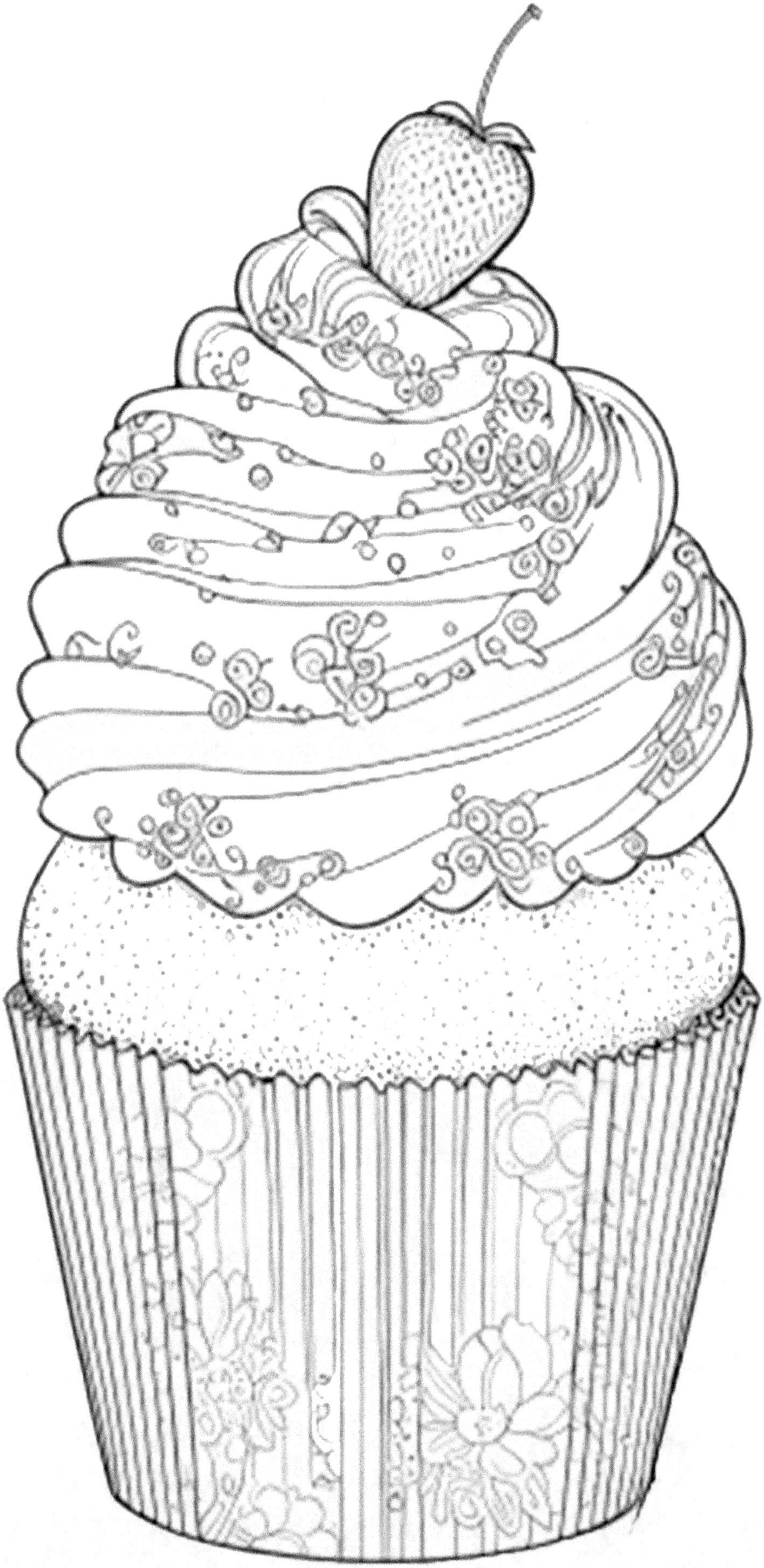

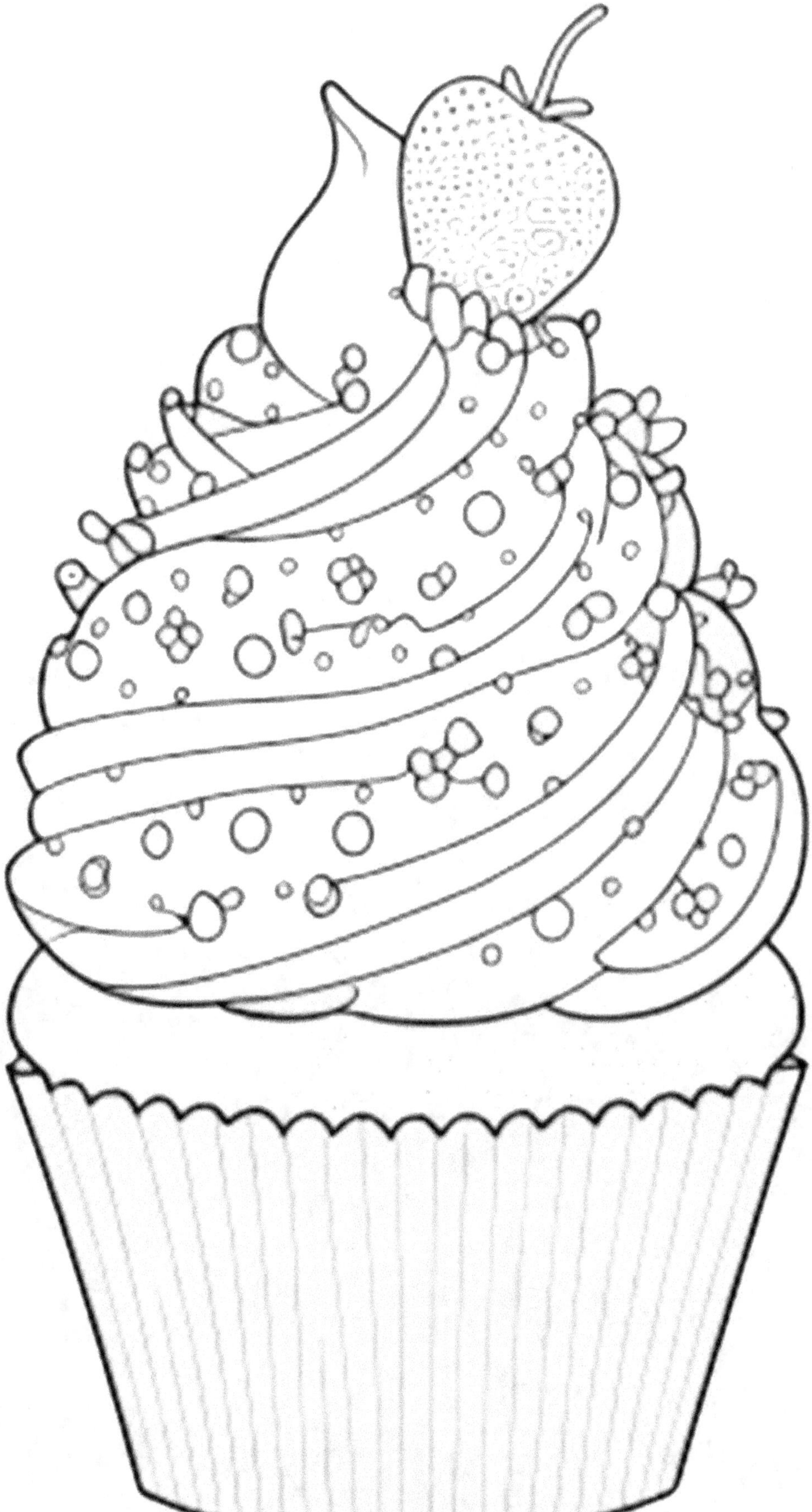

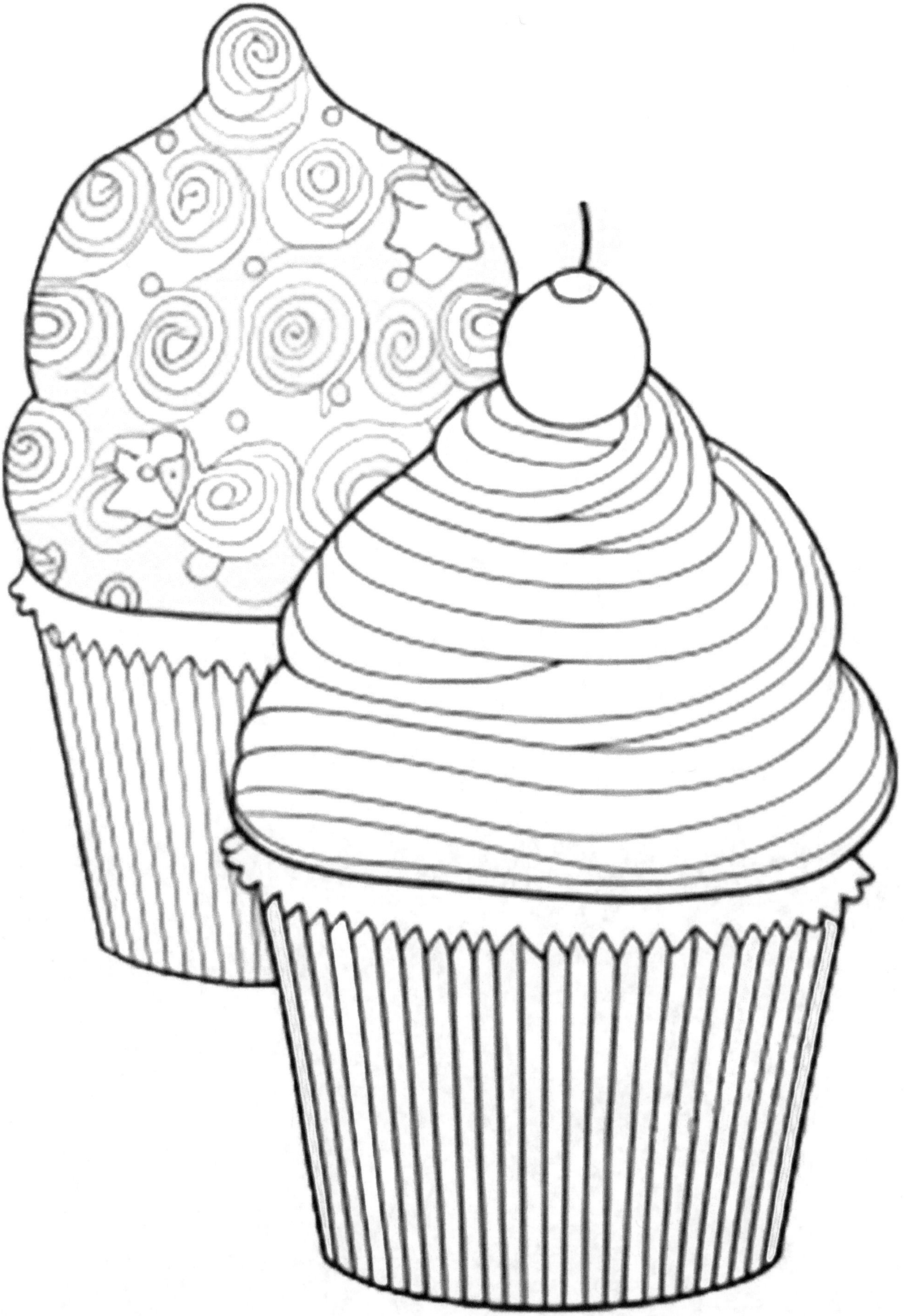

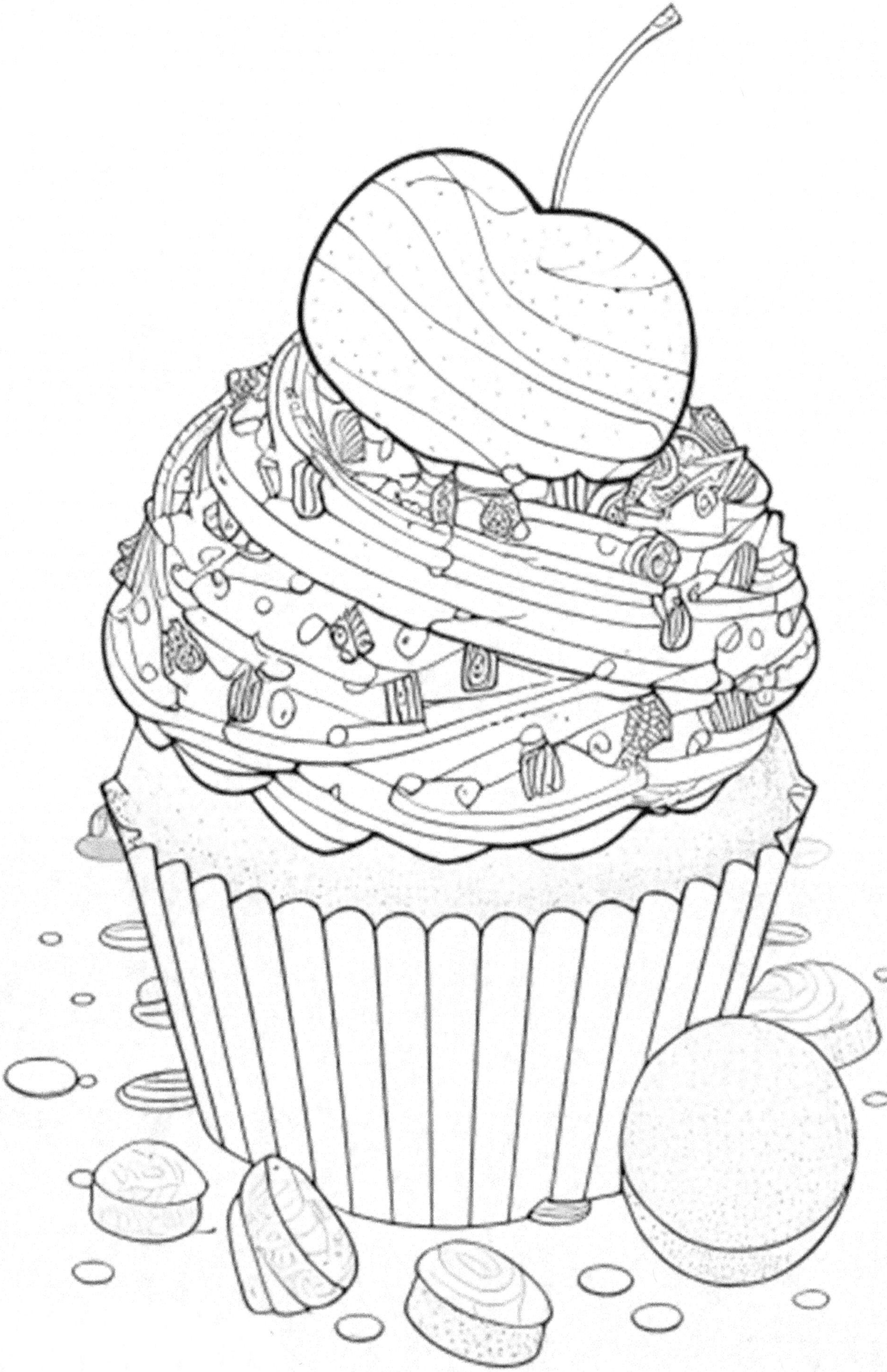

www.ingramcontent.com/pod-product-compliance
Lightning Source LLC
Chambersburg PA
CBHW082152230526
45467CB00044B/3031
* 9 7 9 8 3 7 8 8 3 7 8 9 2 *